Women Welfare and Empowerment

Published by:
Saurabh Publishing House

Women Welfare and Empowerment

A.K. Saxena

Saurabh
Publishing House
4735/22, Prakash Deep Building,
Ansari Road, Daryaganj,
New Delhi- 110002

Published by :
SAURABH PUBLISHING HOUSE

Distributed by :
Lotus Press Publishers & Distributors
Unit No. 220, 2nd Floor, 4735/22, Prakash Deep Building,
Ansari Road, Darya Ganj, New Delhi- 110002
Ph.: 23280047, 09811838000
• E-mail : lotuspress1984@gmail.com
www.lotuspress.co.in

Saurabh Publishing House is an imprint of
Lotus Press Publishers & Distributors

Women Welfare and Empowerment

ISBN: 978-81-89005-47-4 (H/B)

Printed by : **Lotus Press Publishers & Distributors, New Delhi**

Preface

The empowering of women is necessary sustainable development of a community. Sustainability implies a state of balance and equilibrium in factors related to human life which can be social, political, financial, environmental and even spiritual. It is a state to which all those factors that influence the process of the growth of human being and her/his holistic environment has to advance in unison but independently, yet supporting each other. In the case of a woman equality, social justice and freedom have dynamic roles to achieve such sustainability. But the notion of sustainability often become the victim of unsustainable traditions and political opportunism. If a human being is forced to live in an inhuman and degrading condition, sustainable development becomes unattainable. Hence, corruption, nepotism, violence, inequality, exploitation and oppression are counter-productive to sustainable development.

The intimate and probing sharing of ideas with youth and women by our social workers helped us to understand them. Many of the youths believed that certain changes were required for their socio-economic and human development, but they were not quite sure about the quality and quantity of these changes. They were ready for action, but were in need of emotional, intellectual and to a certain extent financial support to achieve their goals. Most of the youths, and a great majority of women were eager to have a better life. The slum dwellers, even though capable of change and growth, were anxious of social change, which might bring about uncertainties.

This book deals with the topics of—*Women after Independence; Status of Women; Women and World; Government and Women Development; Women and Development Process; Basic Concept of Empowerment; Issues of Women Empowerment; Women and Decision-making; Women's Organisation and Empowerment; National Commission for Women; Policies, Programmes for Women Welfare;* etc.

I hope that students and those in the administration field will find it useful for academic and competitive examinations. I owe a deep sense of gratitude to my publisher for materialising my present endeavour.

Author

Contents

1

Women after Independence

Independence inaugurated a new chapter in the history of the struggle for improving the status of Indian Women. The constitution of free India, juridically negated the premise of inequality of women which lay at the heart of the Indian social system. The constitution proclaimed the equal status of woman with man in every aspect. The recognition of juridical equality of Indian women compares favourably with that of women in some of the Third World Countries and also with that of some of the advanced countries where even such juridical equality had not been enunciated.

In pursuance of the principles laid down in the Constitution, a series of legislative enactments have been passed at central and state levels to overcome a number of social disabilities particularly in the area of marriage and property rights. In fact, in India, the major efforts for improving the status of women have been though legislation. It was 1955 when the Hindu Marriage Act was passed. The Act abolished polygamy for Hindus, allowed divorce to either husband or wife on the same grounds and specified the marriage age for girls at fifteen and boys at eighteen, the same age as in the Sarda Act of 1929.

Secular and mixed marriages were legalised by the Special Marriage Act of 1954. These acts were followed by the Hindu Succession Act of 1956, providing that son, daughter and widow mother could inherit equally. In cases of more than one wife, all widows together inherit one share. The Hindu Adoption and Maintenance Bill of 1956 provided separate maintenance for a woman under certain conditions where legal separation or divorce was not sought.

Another remaining problem was (and is) the dowry which is prevalent in most parts of the country. The Dowry Prohibition Act was passed in 1961 in an effort to end this practice. Another major and more recent legislatives effort to improve the position of women has been the passage of state maternity benefit acts, and the Termination of Pregnancy Act in 1972.

It is true that Preamble to the Indian Constitution promises "equality of status and opportunity." However, no comprehensive programme of legislation was undertaken to translate the promise of equality into equality into reality. Since education has spread only in a small section of the community, sufficient public awareness with regard to these laws has not been created. Consequently legislative measures largely remain token gestures on paper *e.g.*, the Special Marriage Act of 1954 and the Hindu Marriage Act of 1955 fixed the minimum age for marriage and declared bigamy unlawful. But child marriage and bigamy still occur in some parts of India. Legislation has also been passed to curb the dowry system (Dowry Prohibition Act, 1961).

Today we see millions of women still suffer because they are women. This granting of equal rights cannot be translated into reality unless the traditional attitudes towards a woman's role in society are altered. Plato once wrote that "as far as the state is concerned there is no difference between natures of men and women." It was because of unequal laws and customs prevailing in the country that differentiate between them. His plea that women ought to be admitted to all the duties and rights of men and his warning regarding the loss to the state as a result of their restricted sphere of activity still remained unheard. And now it has been realised that profound change in the traditional attitudes and customs can only signify a real revolution. It can never be mitiated similar by writing a promise of equality into the Preamble to the constitution or the passing of social legislation. These measures are steps towards equality, to be sure, but in themselves they have not brought about the desired ends.

In India the main focus of most studies on women is their status either at present or through the ages. There are good historical accounts of the status of women in various periods of history based on available records.

Raksha Saran while dealing with the Status of women in the Encyclopaedia of Social Work in India stressed that "In the Vedic age Indian women enjoyed a high status in the home as well as outside. Many of them became distinguished poetesses, mathematicians and theologians—Marriage in those days took place at a fairly advanced age the girls had an effective say in the selection of their husbands.

Rekha Mishra points out in the treatment of the women of Mughal India that "when the Mughal came to India, they continued to treat their ladies with the utmost regard. They often went to pay the respect to them and treated them with all courtesy and kindness and spared no pains to make them comfortable.

Rao provided a sanskritised version of roles and rights of Indian women from the scriptures which is a logical extension of her earlier work on status on women in vedas.

Mukherjee on the basis of a survey on the status of women, sponsored of their right for equal wages for equal work. In rural areas of Tamil Nadu, Haryana and Meghalaya only three percent of the married women were aware of this right. The right for legal abortion was the next least known law in the rural areas. However, the right for inheritance was known to a large percentage of respondents both in Haryana and Tamil Nadu. An overall finding of the study revealed a marked ignorance on the part of women about their own rights. This has an important implication for social change. It is no wonder that social change in India where about 70 percent of the total population still live in villages comes so slowly. To make it speedy, people must be aware of their own rights and duties. If, on the other hand, people do not care to know even about the basic human rights, legislation cannot function as tool for social change; something else is necessary.

Mukherjee has made very significant contribution in the area of status of women. Mukherjee on the basis of the findings of a sample survey conducted in Haryana, Tamil Nadu and Meghalaya reached a number of conclusions regarding the status of women. Despite improvement in the legal status of women over the last century, equal rights and responsibilities were still denied to them. Status in the home was found to be positively related to educational level of the respondent. Substantial proportions of women in the survey were found to be unaware of some of their basic rights. It called for a familiarisation programme. There was no significant relationship between gainful employment status and self-perceived status at home. The final conclusion emerging out of the survey was that although a substantial position of married women were gainfully employed, the traditional definition of the female role has not changed much.

The changing socio-economic status and self-image of women have been studied by Murricken. In an analysis of several studies conducted in three metropolitan centres in Kerala, he concluded that most women in Kerala live under male dominance and were hampered by traditional, cultural and religious taboos. Education by itself was not enough to liberate women. Only a strong mass based movement organised by an enlightened female leadership, he felt, would be able to provide women the freedom and equality to work in partnership with men for their mutual development.

Haksar thought that equal rights for women cannot be had without a fight. It should mean that beginning of an intensive struggle at international, national and personal levels.

Saradmoni repeatedly ventured to state that life cannot be meaningful, rich and full so long as women were confined to home only. Joint participation of men and women in directing and accelerating the socio-economic process in the country would enable a woman to establish something of her inherent inhibitions and weaknesses. To alter the status woman should feel and act like a fully developed independent human being, confident of herself and of her future.

Minattur was of the opinion that radical change in the attitudes of women induced by an awareness of their constitutional rights will be the first step in the complex process of transforming the social structure so that women may enjoy full equality with men in every sphere of life.

Mithan, J. Lani's book published by All India Women's Conference, New Delhi deals with start notes on women's Statutory Rights; Legal Status; Nationality; Marriage and Civil Code; Property and Interstate Succession; Special Marriage Act; Women and Political Rights; Social Status; Women's Education; Public Health; Family Planning and Women's Employment. It also gives a note on the Indian Women's Charter of Rights and Duties. "The Charter demands for its working women that:

(a) There should be no bar to the employment of married and unmarried women provided they are prepared to abide by the conditions of service;

(b) No woman shall be debarred owing to sex from the enjoyment offull equality regarding social and labour rights and duties, both men and women shall equally receive special consideration on grounds of health and in the case of women on grounds of motherhood;

(c) While women workers with regard to pay which should be a living wage, leave, hours of work, sickness allowance, holidays with pay and free medical treatment, and snail have the same amenities with regard to bathrooms, lavatories, canteens serving hot meals etc., they shall be allowed special facilities by way of *(i)* cretches for their babies and nursery schools; *(ii)* rest rooms for expectant and nursing mothers; *(iii)* milk canteens for the children nursing and expectant mothers; *(iv)* a break during work for expectant and nursing mothers; and *(v)* maternity benefits which shall form part of a comprehensive scheme of social insurance.

All these studies indicate that theoretically and legaly women are recognised as the social equal to men. But in reality they are still in the grip of traditional roles and have not freed themselves from the dominance of men. In order to free them from this situation, the women should understand their rights, should become economically independent and should improve their standard of living.

Social Network

Sociology from its earliest days, has been concerned with the ways in which the social relations between people constitute a distinct reality. This reason of social structure was seen as produced through the intersection of chains of action and their unintended consequences. While classical sociologistr may have disagreed among themselves on the question of whether such structures were reducible, in principle, to the constituent social actions of the people who produced them, there was a general agreement that social structure had distinct and important properties which provided the basic subject matter of the discipline of sociology.

It was, perhaps, in classical German sociology that this viewpoint was most explicitly allied with the metaphor of a 'network' of social relations; the social world being depicted as an intertwined mesh of connections through which individuals were bound together. The very language used is redolent of the production of fabrics and textiles, and the works of Tonnies, Weber and above all Simmel abound with concept's embodying with such language: chains of action 'interweave and interlock' to form a tight 'knit' social 'fabric'.

The first true formulations of social network analysis, in which the metaphor was taken seriously as the basis for developing a set of sociological concepts, took place in social psychology. During 1930s, Moreno began to develop what he called 'sociometry' as a way of conceptualising the structures of small groups produced through friendship patterns and informal interactions. The stars of social interaction those who received a large number of friendship choices from others were dramatically depicted in Moreno's 'sociogram' as the hubs of radiating patterns of lines, each line representing a friendship choice directed from one person to another. Through the use of such diagram, Moreno was able to develop the metaphor of network into a fruitful, but still rudimentary, sociological concept. Bavelas and Festinger considerably enlarged their work and laid the foundations for the study of 'group dynamics' which comprised the backbone of American social psychology in the mid-twentieth century.

There are several concepts which have been used to designate relations between the people. These are the concepts of 'net', 'relation', 'web', 'network', etc. A net refers to connections between several lines of relations in the context of a society or a group. Mitchell writes, "A network in a graphic theory is a relation in which the lines connecting the points have values ascribed to them, which mayor may not be numerical". In sociological studies the word 'network' is applied to somewhat differentiated structure distinguished in graph theory. In sociology, one has to think of an identificable set of persons and the relationships that exist between them. This is known as 'diagraphic notion' of relations. While elaborating social structure, anthropologist Radcliffe Brown in his presidential address to the Royal Anthropological Society remarked that 'social network, the fundamental tool of social anthropology is now receiving increased acceptance throughout the social sciences'.

Although the concept of social network is used here in a metaphorical sense and is not tied to any analytical framework, Radcliffe Brown does succeed in focusing our attention on patterns in the interactions and interpersonal relations of individuals. And he declares openly his belief that these repeated patterns have important substantive significance in themselves. This is an important point of view. For Radcliffe Brown societal social structure is built up from individual pairs of interpersonal interactions, while the social structure simultaneously imposes constraints on which interactions can take place.

Nadel uses the term network, though in a different way. He equates it to system. He says that it is through, abstracting from the concrete population and its behaviour the pattern network (or system) of relationships', existing between role playing actors that social structure is arrived at. He lays stress on network of relationship as basic structure, *i.e.* how relationships are structured and mapped. It is the interlocking of relationships through the dichotomisation of roles which brings about an expansion of the areas of relationships into networks. These can be open ended as well as bounded sub-groups whose systematic interrelation makes up the social structure. Nadel stresses that both kinds of network exist in a society but he is more interested in the latter and, therefore, devotes little attention to the openended network.

Barnes idea of social network is the first major advance in sociology since 'role'. The aspect of Barnes analysis which has received most attention is his view of the network. It is the definition of network that formed the first step in his analysis. Barnes introduced the idea of social network to describe an order of social relationships to understand social behaviours. Barnes studied the ties among members of a Norwegian community as the class system. But sensitised to the importance of face to face social relations as they result from the organisation of society, Barnes examines how class features express themselves at the local level, the level of acquaintance and friendship ties. Social class lines are defined by the equivalence relations expressed by individuals in the community who share symmetric pairs of relations and who accord each other approximately equal status.

For Barnes, 'network' does not predicate more than that certain relationship interlock through persons participating in more than one relationship, whereas for Nadal, it is a situation in which this interlocking also bears on 'what happens' in the relationship and hence on their effective interdependence. For Barnes, the important thing is the dispersal of the relationship and open ended character of the network; for Nadel, it is coherence and closure, that is, its equivalence.

Mitchell's comment on Barnes formulation is: 'This step whereby the relationship of the linkages in a network to one another is taken to be a salient factor in interpreting social action is one of the steps whereby the metaphor of a social network is expanded into an analogy and made analytically useful'.

Grieco Margaret in her study: Keeping it in the Family: Social Networks and Employment Change, stressed upon the role kin networks play in the social organisation of employment. She explored, how family relationships are relevant to the employment chances ofthe individual. Unlike Granovetter who considered weak ties as crucial for getting information about employment, she argued that the economic chances of the individual are strongly affected by his or her membership of a particular kinship group.

The existence of total network is not denied by anyone. Total networks are such as are not defined by selection of a particular person or group as the focal point or ego. Barnes conceives of a total network as 'inter-connected chain or system of immaterial things'. It has no units or boundaries, it has no coordinating organisation. It is made up of the ties of friendship and acquaintance. Some of the ties are between kinsmen. Each person as it were, is in touch with each other and some of whom are not. Both of them also included both kinds of relationship direct and finite.

Public awareness of women's real issues such as gender equality economic and public participation and equal rights in terms of land and property etc., increased tremendously in the last two decades, especially during the U.N. Women's Decad in 1976-85. Several activities, programmes towards women's emancipation have been attempted by individual workers, governmental and non-governmental agencies and universities as well. But the outcome of these efforts is limited to a few pockets and issues, leaving enormous scope for further work.

Empowering women may be understood as enabling women to acquire and possess power resources, in order, for them to make decisions on their own or resist decisions that are made by others which affect them. A person may be said to be powerful when he/she has control over a greater or equal proportion of power resources in society. The extent of possession of various power resources, such as personal wealth, assets, land, skills, education, information, knowledge, social status, position, leadership traits, capabilities for mobilisation and manoeuvrability etc., determines the degree of decision-making power. Women, especially in rural areas, possess least proportion of these resources and as a result they are powerless and dependent on men, throughout the whole network. He also gives examples of 'partial networks', the cognetic web of kinship, network of marriage, political networks and religions networks. He further holds that networks could be total or partial and both could be finite or infinite and bounded or unbounded.

Whitten and Wolf suggested' freezing of time' as an important dimension of social network. As the researcher begins to work with real data rather than abstractly conceived relationships, he discovers, once again, that relationships exist in time and change through time. For the construction of theory one must add a time by which the network is limited. Social relationships link us backward in time ultimately forward into future. Social networks are an ongoing processes, they may change with time and situation. Researchers have to keep 'time' and 'situation' variability so as to pinpoint the structural dimension of social networks.

When one encounters an empirical reality, one is convinced that the mobilisation of people is related to the social situation. A person may be mobilised by an ego in one social situation and may refuse to be mobilised in another. These uncertainties in the mobilisation of people mainly arising out of social situations, create the problems of boundary of personal networks as well as of continuity of the relationship between the members of network.

Action sets and personal or ego-centric networks have been suggested by anthropologists for devoting limited networks. The term 'action set' could be retained for analysing the links between individuals in specific situations. In this respect the observation of Mitchell is relevant. He says, "At one extreme there are the links in the action set which are mobilised to cope with a particular crisis. At the other extreme there are networks which are in constant use and are the means for innumerable transactions before and after the "I" specific incident which is the point of analysis, Boissevain looks at 'personal' or 'ego-centric' network from the standpoint of the ego. He means by 'social or personal network', the chains of persons with whom a given ego is in actual contact or with whom he can enter into contact. The personal network or each person is distinct although it may touch and very often overlap that of others with greater emphasis on ego. Mitchell holds that, 'a network is most conveniently anchored on an individual'. Mayer on the other hand, looks at the term 'set' (similar to 'personal network') from the angle of the alters in a network or set, when he says that, 'the component units of a set have a known boundary, it not one of group membership but of their common connection to the central ego'. The fact remains that these two approaches to the conceptualisation of personal or ego-centric networks, *i.e.*, looking at networks either from the angle of ego or that of alters, raise a number of questions. The questions involve the meaning of the terms like 'contact', 'common connection' centrality of the ego, etc . Apart from this, the significance of recruitment or of mobilisation of the members of personal network by an ego for the relatively enduring relationships beyond a specific situation has also to be explored. The centricity of ego adds a new dimension to the analysis of networks. A person has meaningful contacts with several persons on the basis of which a network emerges. There can be two angles of looking at the centricity of ego, *i.e.*, 'sociometric' and 'methodological'. The logic in sociometric is that an individual may be the focal point of any network in a specific situation as it is done in leadership studies, whereas from the methodo-logical point, we may study the network, starting from any point which it becomes the centre as it is done to trace lineage in genealogical studies. But the important thing here is that an individual may or may not be the centre of his network. In fact, there need not be any centre. Anyone of the members may activate or mobilise others and at the time of mobilisation he may be considered the centre of the network and thus centres may shift from one action set to another. The upshot of the analysis is that we should distinguish between non-ego-centric personal networks and ego centric personal network.

Micro-Macro Analysis

The interrelationships of macro and micro level theory and data are a concern of all social and behavioural sciences that study both individuals and collectivities like organisations, nations and firms. The basic problem is to explain how persons affect collectivities and how collectivities affect persons over time. However, to conceptualise and measure reciprocal effects over time is a formidable undertaking. We are only at the beginning of this task.

Reviewing the history of the problem in sociology as to set the argument in the proper context we find that few scholars debated macro and micro relations until the 1960s when Homans tried to reduce sociology to social behaviourism. His attack on macro sociology was joined by interpretive sociologists (who with a few notable exceptions) tended not to share Homans view of the requirements of scientific research. Their theories tended to be radically anti-collectivist, and they were being attacked for failing to take social structure into account. The actor was not seen as bringing a previously defined collective order into play. Much of the ensuing discussion was conducted by militant micro-sociology as a war against macro-sociology.

During most of the twentieth century, macro sociologists paid little attention to the controversy because, first, it seemed irrelevant. As Goffman said, social organisations and structure could be studied quite nicely without reference to social psychology. Macro theory must account for patterns of social relations not on the basis of motives but on the basis of external constraints and opportunities for social relations created by population composition and the structure of positions in social environment.

Second, the controversy was muddled by disagreement about the meaning of the words Micro and Macro. Everyone agreed that micro refers to something small. Beyond this, sociologists divided into two camps. One camp included interpretive sociologists, who tended to equate macro with 'quantitative' and micro with 'qualitative' sociology. This definition puts their own work, based on individual data, in the micro category but it implicitly excludes other works based on individual data (status attainment, for example), when those data are collected with methods that involve a quantitative and qualitative mix like that of survey research. To our knowledge, no other scholars of social and behavioural science use these words. As Berger, Eyre and Zeldith point out, it is wrong to use micro to mean a small unstructured action system while macro refers to a large unstructured system without action. This treats the analytic aspects of micro and macro theories as being correlated when in fact they are independent and raise fruitless questions about relationships. The other camp includes everyone else: macro sociologists, exchange theorists, life course theorists, and so on. Whatever else they disagree about, they tend to equate micro with individual and macro with collective level events. Some sociologists in this large residual category see the problem as one of showing how micro affects macro in a theoretical generalising way. For sociologists, the natural unit of observation has been the individual. Thus the analysis must move from the individual level of observation to the system level where problems of interest usually lie. But how to move remains an unsolved problem that requires the integration of exchange theory and macrostructure. The extent to which the problem can be solved remains to be seen. Other sociologists have taken a macro to micro approach. One fruitful example is the life course perspective. It mixes history, social psychology, and demography with powerful quantitative techniques that can now handle both the timing and sequencing of events. Life course theorists examine Cohort and period effects on individuals with data taken from historical demography, social history and recent longitudinal studies. These studies necessarily focus only on the industrial era because they require data that can be analysed quantitatively.

Peter Blau shifted his concern from micro level to more macro one in which he suggested that macro structural theory should be built on the basis of micro-sociological theory but later on he abandoned his own exchange theory because it could not cope with the properties of population and collectivities.

Blau stressed that both the theories, that is, micro and macro are fundamentally different because they look at social relations from opposite perspectives. One might say, speaking metaphorically, that exchange theory examines social relations from within whereas macro structural theory examines them from without. The former dissects the exchange processes assumed to underlie all social relations and gives them their feature and dynamics; whatever the broader social system in which they are embedded; it is a micro but a general theory like micro economics. Macro structural theory analyses the structural framework consisting of the population composition that limits and governs the social relations that can develop regardless of cultural norms and individual desires and thereby shapes the patterns or structures of social relations in communities and otner large collectivities.

Although exchange theory and macro structural theory view a phenomena from a different standpoint, they are not contradictory to each other. Merton has stressed the significance of pluralistic theories in a discipline for the advancement of knowledge. Different subject matter often require explanations by different theories, at least in the early stages of the development of a discipline, notwithstanding the ultimate goal of integrating the various theories, in accordance with the Ocean's razor. These theories are complementary in the sense that what one takes as given and postulates as an assumption without trying to explain it, the other treats as problematical and seeks to explain. The micro sociological focus is appropriate for the study of entire societies or other large collectivities, because it is impossible to trace and dissect the interpersonal relations of many thousands or millions or people, and neither would it be meaningful if all were described.

The micro sociological approach, pointing a large canvas, cannot explain these processes, because it does not investigate interpersonal relations in depth. For example, the existence of in-group tendencies is assumed by the macro structural theory but the processes producing them are not explained. Exchange theory seeks to explain them by noting how similarities in background, experience and social position make it likely that people exchange mutual support for their opinions and conduct, furnishing incentives for social interaction. Moreover, in-group preferences, such as people's values generally have two manifestations. They induce persons to associate with members of their own group themselves and they also induce them to approve of others who choose in group associates and to disapprove of those who choose outsiders. These exchange processes sustain and reinforce the in-group pressures assumed to exist by macro-structural theory. According to this theory, however, structural conditions may constrain persons to engage increasingly in inter group relations. Such greater prevalence of inter-group relations implies that in-group pressures are weakened because when many persons are involved in inter-group relations, these are no longer widely disapproved. Here again exchange theory can explain the diminished in-group pressures by the lesser approved people earn for confining their relations to the ingroup. And while micro and macro theorising are complementary, they are nevertheless about different subject matter.

The further extension of exchange theory, from dyadic to more macro was the major concern of Richard, M. Emerson. He is one of the key figures in the development of social exchange theory in sociology.

Emerson's theoretic approach liberated exchange theory from the conceptual shackles of behaviourism and utilitarianism. In doing so, it allowed the analysis of social structure. This was a major breakthrough indeed, ill extending exchange theory from dyadic concerns to the analysis of larger groups where the study of structure becomes meaningful. Instead of asking why an actor finds something rewarding and enters into a social relation, Emerson tended to ask: Given a social relation, how can its form and dynallics be explained in terms of exchange theoretic concepts? If actors form exchange relations, then it is assumed that they find it rewarding. The important sociologist questions then revolve around the form of the relation, once it exists.

According to Emerson, 'most exchange theory, however, fails to deal effectively with social systems larger than the dyad'. His theoretical formulation stresses on individual action based on a coherent set of operant principles of behaviour. Having developed a sound conception of individual action as a building block, he goes on to articulate a more general theory of social interaction linking actors involved in social exchange relation together to form structures, network or corporate group.

Using a small set of concepts drawn from operant psychology, Emerson introduces a definition of an 'organism-environment', exchange relation that identifies the smallest independently meaningful unit in terms of which large structures are conceptualised. Key concepts include opportunities, initiations and transactions. These terms are defined using operant terminology. For instance, an opportunity in a stimulus situation which contains appropriate discriminative stimuli, for evolving an initiation. Initiations are defined as 'operant responses' and transactions as positively 'reinforced initiations'. Opportunities invoke initiations which mayor may not result in transactions. Initiations are a function of two factors: *(a)* the existence of an opportunity and *(b)* the degree of 'satiation-deprivation' for a specific resource on a particular occasion.

The fundamental concept, exchange relation implies a continuing series of opportunities, initiations and transactions, not isolated events. In Emerson's words, "this, concept links each transaction to a history and a future for specific actors emphasising a more or less durable social relation between actors (A and B with behaviour X and Y) significantly modifiable across time". These relations and the conditions under which they form, change and break are the focus of Emerson's theory. Exchange theory from tautology by dealing to examine how, given a social relation can its from and dynamics be explained in terms of exchange theoretic concepts. A shift away from a study of individual behaviour to a study of social relations proved a major landmark in the development of exchange theory. Furthermore, by merging exchange theory and network analysis. Emerson was able to fill the conceptual gap that existed between micro-sociology and macro-sociology.

The formal treatment of individual level action concludes with the introduction of three important notions: exchange domains, alternative relations and dependence. Actors unlike Skinner's rats, are assumed to have choice or decision points (actually, even Skinner's rats face choice points). Actors thus have a variety of opportunities and can be conceived as connected to a set of possible exchange relations (*i.e.*, opportunities to obtain valued resources from various personal and non-personal sources.) It is the existence of alternatives that is the key factor in defining dependence. Alternatives are defined as relations within the same exchange domain; that is they offer 'substitutable' resources or meet the same needs for the actor. For Emerson the concept of an exchange domain employs the criterion of satiation as behavioural basis for defining the boundaries between classes of re-inforcers. Domains, he argues can be thought of as 'points of articulation' between an actor's 'needs or values' and sectors of the environment. Uncertainty or the 'degree to which exchange is problematic' is introduced as the factor that determines the value of outcomes, both within and across domains. Finally, exchange relations are characterised in this formulation by primacy. Simply put, primacy represents the extent to which a given relation mediates a range of valued outcomes or domains for any given actor.

●●●

2

Status of Women

With the break-through in science, emergence of reform movements and philosophers and thinkers propagating concepts like equality and freedom a questioning to the position of women, her role and status in society also started. The 20th century in particular promoted the cause of gender justice by internationalising struggles for equality by women and other oppressed people. Women's struggles against their subordination were intertwined in varying degrees with ideologies and movements based on the values of freedom, self-determination, equality, democracy and justice. Confined earlier by local or limited foci, these now found expression through movements against imperialism, for national liberation and social transformation. As a result the biological basis of sex role stereotypes, economic and social base of women's status, power relations and other related gender issues have become not only subjects of study but also for movements for change, assertion and justice. These came to Indian also first as a part of national movement and then as issues in development after independence. In last two decades or so these have become significant both in tenns of studies and women's development and movements.

Anthropological studies in various parts of the world point out to a wide variation in male and female roles across cultures and demonstrate the possibility of change in these sex determined roles. There is little physical determinism about which gender performs which role apart from pregnancy and child birth. In this context status and position of women in India, has also not been same always.

The relationship between the sexes during the earliest period of our history—the Vedic Age (before 1000 BC)—was characterised by a reciprocity in which the right and obligations of each were nearly equivalenced. Sex norms were liberal and marriages though valued was not obligatory. Neither the Rig Veda nor the Brihya Sutras enjoined any kind of binding obedience of the wife to her husband. She was free to participate in all religious practices and sacrifices and was 'entitled to all the samskaras' or religious sacraments like men; and not only were religious prayers and sacrifices jointly offered by the husband and the wife, but the wife alone could offer them in the absence of her husband.

During Aryan consolidation from 1000 BC onwards, particularly in north India several drastic changes took place in Hindu society which led to the curtailment of the freedom of women. With the consolidation of Aryan power a vast majority of subjects were non-Aryan people. The Aryans married the non-Aryans women. But non-Aryan women were prohibited from participating in religious rituals. Gradually all women, Aryan as well as non-Aryan became ineligible for Vedic studies and religious duties. The code of Manu combined with the Shrutikaras and Smritikars. Nath Upnishad and Shankaracharya launched the sexual apartheid in Indian society. The Muslim conquest of India in 900 AD introduced the Purdah system and further pushed women deep into domesticity. During the Muslim rule the percentage of literacy among women went down rapidly. *Sati* also became prevalent along with religious ban on the widow remarriage.

In general the Indian society like a number of "classical" societies was patriarchal. Patriarchal values regulating sexuality, reproduction and social production prevailed and were expressed through specific cultural metaphors. Overt rules prohibiting women from specific activities and denying certain rights did exist. But more subtle expression of patriarchy was through symbolism giving messages of inferiority of women through legends highlighting the self-sacrificing, self-effacing pure image of women and through the ritual practices which day in and day out emphasised the dominant role of a women as a faithful wife and devout mother. The basic rules for women's behaviour as expressed in the Laws of Manu insist that a women must constantly worship her husband as a God, even though he is destitute of virtue or a womaniser. Women should be kept in dependency by her husband because by nature they are passionate and disloyal.

The contradictions introduced into Hinduism also gave rise to disenchantments and periodic protects and revolts. Thus, Buddhism, Jainism, the Bhagati Movement, Islam, Veerasaivism, Sikhism, Christianity—all testify to the need felt by large sections of the Indian society for more satisfactory alternative to the existing socio-religious orders of the day. In each of these religions, except perhaps Islam, the position of women marginally improved. But it was not until the impact of western liberalism had made itself felt through English education that reform movements really launched their crusades.

It was during the British colonial period after coming into contact with the English education and in some cases as a reaction to British rule there sprang up many reformist movements in India. Brahmo Samaj, Arya Samaj, Prartha Samaj and many other movements took up the cause of injustice against women. As a well known the early reformist Raja Ram Mohan Roy denounced child marriage, and sati and worked for the emancipation of women in general. The nineteenth century also saw for the first time the enactment of social legislation by the government which included abolition of Sati (1829), Widow Remarriage Act (1856), Civil Marriage Act (1872). Another significant feature of the nineteenth century is the attempts towards girls education.

In Nationalist movement also the Indian women's immense hidden potential found a forum for its release. Gandhiji called on women to give up Purdah and participate in Politics. In 1917 a women's delegation met the Secretary of State for India to demand franchise for women. In 1927 was launched All India Women's Conference for the welfare and development of women.

While as a result of social reforms and nationalist movement there emerged awareness about women's plight and consciousness for their upliftment in general there was not much change in the social attitude towards women, particularly in rural areas. Also inspite of some significant social legislature, property, inheritance and such laws remained against women.

Legal Equality for Women

The National Movement leaders had not only called upon the women to participate in the freedom struggle as equals but have also committed themselves to the ideology of gender equality. In the Fundamental Rights Resolution of the Indian National Congress adopted in 1931. It was postulated "freedom, justice, dignity and equality for women was essential for nation-building". The framers of the Constitution of India, therefore, tried to give proper place to the women in the social structure of the country. In the Preamble of the Constitutional the solemn resolve of the founding fathers contain two specific objectives which have a direct bearing on the status of women:

(a) Justice.... Social, economic and political for all.

(b) Equality.... of status and opportunity for all.

Parts III and IV of the Constitution dealing with Fundamental Rights and Directive Principles elaborate these declarations in concrete forms. In chapter on Fundamental Rights, Article 14 envisages that the State shall not deny to any person equality before the law or equal protection of law. Article 15 specifically prohibits discrimination on grounds such as caste, religion and sex. Article 16 provides for the equality of opportunity in matters relating to public employment. The Constitution at the same time gives power to the state to make special provisions for women and children. The inclusion of this provision makes it possible for the state to enact legislature for the welfare of women even if that violates Fundamental Rights in general.

The chapter on Directive Principles apart from directing the state to work for the socio-economic betterment of society provides four women-specific directives:

(i) Men and women equality have the right to an adequate means of livelihood. (Article 39a)

(ii) There is equal pay for equal work for both men and women. (Article 39cd)

(iii) The health and strength of workers men and women and the tender age of children are not abused and that citizens are not forced by econotnic necessity to enter avocations unsuited to their age or strength. (Article 39e)

(iv) Make provision for just and humane conditions of work and maternity relief.

Apart from these negative and positive obligations on the state the Constitution also (after the 42nd Amendment 1976) imposes a fundamental duty on all citizens. "to renounce practices derogatory to the dignity of women" (Article 51A). As mentioned earlier the Constitution of India has also granted universal franchise. Thus women has equality both in right to vote and contest elections.

Besides providing a formal structure of equality through the Constitution. the Government has also been using law as a major instrument for change and development. Right from the time of achievement of Independence, Jawaharlal Nehru in particular, initiated legislature with a view to remove disparities with regard to women. Thus various Acts like Special Marriage Act 1954, the Hindu Marriage Act 1955, the Hindu Minority and Guardianship Act, 1956 the Hindu Adoption and Maintenance Act 1956, Suppression of Immoral Traffic in Women Act 1956 and Dowry Prohibition Act 1961 were enacted.

A major initiative in legislature field was taken in 1970s and 1980s particularly after the submission of report by the Committee on the status of women in India (1975) and emergence of women's movements and organisations.

Some of the important enactments in this regard include the Medical Termination of Pregnancy Act 1971, the Equal Remuneration Act 1976, the Child Marriage Restraint (Amendment) Act 1978 and the Criminal law (Amendment) Act 1983, the Family Courts Act, 1984, The Criminal Law (Second Amendment Act) 1985, The Dowry Prohibition (Amendment) Act 1984. Through these acts the discrimination against women on the grounds of sex in the matter of employment has been removed, the age for marriage for girls has been raised to 18 years, the onus of proof in cases of rape has been shifted to offender and punishment for rape has been made stringent, cruelty to a women by her husband or in-laws has been made punishable. In addition to enactment of laws by the legislature the Judiciary also has been interpreting some existing laws in more favourable ways for women. In a landmark judgement in November 1995 the

Supreme Court gave the widow and daughter of a deceased equal right to property left by him. Earlier in two other cases the Supreme Court granted a divorced Hindu Women the right to sell, use for income or dispose in any way she likes land given to her in lieu of maintenance, and gave the widow full ownership rights on the residence given to her as part of maintenance.

Welfare Programmes

The efforts towards women's development and gender justice have not been limited to enactment and favourable interpretation of laws. It has also been recognised and realised that women need access to inputs like education, skill development, management, training and gender sensitisation. For this efforts have been made by the government for inclusion of women's development in Five Year Plans. The approach to women's development in First Plan was included in Community Development Programme. The Third and Fourth Five Year Plans accorded a high priority to education and welfare of women. The Fifth Plan shifted approach from welfare of women to the development of women. In the Sixth Five Year Plan there was a major thrust on health, education and employment of women. A separate department of women and child development was set up at the centre in 1985 to give a distinct identity and provide a nodal point on matters relating to women's development. The Seventh Five Year Plan emphasised on the need to open new avenues of work for women and perceived them as a crucial resources for the development of the country. The Eighth Plan marks a further shift in its approach from Development to Empowerment of Women. Later in the ninth, tenth and eleventh plan the government take bold steps for the improvement regarding empowerment of women in many ways.

The Government of India in 1953 also established a Central Social Welfare Board with a nation-wide programme of grants-in-aid, for promoting welfare and development services for women, children and under privileged groups. The Board has its state counterparts. This programme of the government on the one hand encouraged growth of a large number of women's organisations and on the other hand provided status and activity to many of the erstwhile active women social or political workers. Proliferation of Mahila Mandals is a striking phenomenon of this. Many State governments have also made provisions for free education for girls upto secondary or in some cases even university education. Family planning and welfare programmes are also targeted towards improvement of women.

Inspite of freedom and equality granted to women in terms of participation and contest of elections women's share in elected decision making bodies had remained not only low but in many cases negligible. For this an initiative was taken in 1988 for reservation of seats for women in local self government bodies. 73rd and 74th Constitutional Amendments passed in 1992 have provided for 33 per cent reservation of seats at various levels of Panchayati Raj bodies and Municipalities. Same is now proposed for Parliament and State Legislatures.

India has also been participant in programmes for women's development undertaken at international level and has also signed covenants and declarations at these for it may be pointed here that in the post second world war period there had been consistent efforts in this direction at various international fora, important of these are mentioned below.

In 1945 United Nations adopted Article 8 of the character pledging non-discrimination against women; "in any capacity and under conditions of equality" in all UN bodies. In 1946 was established the Commission on the status of women. This commission has drafted declarations and conventions, monitored and highlighted issues on a spectrum of issues and served as secretariat for major conferences on women issues. In 1967 the Declaration on the Elimination of All Forms of Discrimination Against Women was adopted. It called for recognition of equality for women in fact as well as in law. In 1972 UN General Assembly designated 1975 as the International Women's year to focus on women's issue and in the international Women's year at the first conference on women at Mexico was adopted "World Plan of Action" and also proclaimed first decade for women with the themes of equality, development and peace. The General Assembly in 1976 established voluntary fund for women. In 1985 this was broadened to become UN Development Fund for Women. The second conference on women was held in Copenhagen in 1980 and the Third in Nairobi in 1985. This Conference adopted the forward looking strategies for the Advancement of women to the year 2000. The UN Conference on Environment and Development held in 1992 recognised that women were not only the most adversely affected victims of environmental devastation and social change but also the most potent agents for change. The world conference on Human Rights held in Vienna in 1993 integrated violence against women and other women's human rights issues into the overall UN human rights agenda. m 1994, the international Conference on Population and Development for the first time recognised that gender equity and the empowerment of women through education, health and nutrition were linked to traditional population issues such as family planning. The Fourth World Conference on women in Beijing held in 1995, reviewed and debated 12 critical areas of concern and adopted a new "Platform For Action."? In June 2000 was held Beijing plus five at UN headquarters at New York to stake stock of the progress since Beijing India is a party to all these.

Status of Women

The term status denotes position of an individual in a social system; it also encompass in itself the notions of rights and obligations, of superiority and inferiority, in terms of power authority and grading. In the context of women, status implies :What is her position in a particular sub-system? What are her rights and privileges? How are they determined? Does she have access to power, authority and privileges? How does her status compare with that of men? How has her position been changed?

In this context Centre for Women's Development studies brings out the evidence of growing inequalities and vulnerabilities of women in all sectors—economic, social demographic, health, nutrition, etc. The process of development, instead of reducing inequalities based on divisions like caste, class, gender "religion and ethnicity have at time strengthened these. Some of these forces have their roots in old obscurantist traditions which are trying to reassert themselves like widow burning, while some represent new sociopolitical forces which seek to avert sectional identities at the cost of women's rights and constitutional goals. The centre brings out the status of women on the basis of four indicators—demographic, literacy, economic and social.

(1) Demographic Declining Sex-ratio. Normal demographic distribution in most countries demonstrates a slightly higher number of women. In India, however, the sex-ratio (number of women per 1000 men) kept declining for well over hundred years with no change in the trend till 1981. According to 1991 census the sex ration was 927 women per 1000 men but the recent survey (2007) showed decline in the lower ration of 880.

Sex ratio is an indicators of health, nutrition and survival status of women and girl children. Several factors contribute to this imbalance.

(a) Bias and discrimination against the girl child and preference for the male child leading to higher female

infant mortality due to neglect, malnutrition and inadequate access to health care.

(*b*) Preference for sons, leading to misuse of amniocentesis (sex determination tests) and selective abortion of female foetuses. Female infanticide is reported to be on the increase in some areas. There is an expression of systematic bias against girls and misuse of scientific knowledge and tools.

(*c*) Over work and malnutrition and repeated pregnancies among women in poor households leading to higher maternal mortality, morbidity and low expectancy.

(2) Literacy Rates. One of the major changes which has occurred during this century is the importance given to education of women. But inspite of various plans, schemes and programmes education for girls has not showed the desired results. The female literacy rate in 1991 was 39.29 as against 64.13 for males. The literacy rate among men has gone up from 24.95 in 1951 to 64.13 in 1991. While for women it has increased from 7.9 to 39.29 in the same period. The latest female literacy rate in 2002 increased upto 9 percent approximately and the recent trends of government shows another 5 percent increase in the literacy rate. The literacy rates are uniformly low among women in rural areas and particularly among Scheduled Castes and Scheduled Tribes. While the overall literacy rates have improved paradoxically, the number of illiterate women has also increased over the decades due to population growth, non-enrolment of girls and drop-outs from the formal system of education. In absolute terms the number of illiterate women has increased from 153.7 million to 241.7 million. Besides literacy, even if one looks at the progress of education at various levels, not only the rate of progress is very slow, but there is a wide gap between the education of boys and girls at all stages. In school education the enrolment of girls has been increasing, but due to various socio-economic factors the drop-out rate is schooling. As per a Union Education Ministry report, 74 per cent of the girls in the 6-14 age groups quit school before completion of education.

Illiteracy and lack of education among women limits their achievements in the field of employment, training and utilisation of health facilities. It is also negatively related with fertility rates and infant and child mortality rates. According to National Family Health Survey 1992-93 the age of marriage increases sharply with the education of women. Among women age 25-29 the medium age at marriages rises from 15.3 years for illiterate women to 21.7 years for women who have completed high school.

(3) Economy and Employment. Constitutional rights, expansion of economy, industrialisation and urbanisation have all opened various opportunities for women's employment and sectoral balances. The census evidence, however, shows that there are marginal changes in the employment of women by economic sectors. Even these marginal changes suggest that women when compared to men, are lumped into low paying or unpaid work. The number of women employed in the organised sector has increased from 13.7 lakhs in 1962 to 35.7 lakhs in 1989. This represents an increase in the women's share in employment in the organised sector from 1.3 per cent to 13.7 per cent in 1989, which is substantial.

Both National Sample Survey and the Census data show that women make up about 44 per cent of the agricultural wage workers. It has also been observed that almost all rural women are involved to some extent in agriculture. The nature and extent of their involvement varies widely and is also strongly influenced by the economic status, caste and ethnic background of the family. Female agricultural labourers are indeed among the poorest in India, with the lowest wage level and highest unemployment. 61 per cent of them are below poverty line.

Estimates of the average hours of unpaid work done by women outside their homes vary from 6.1 to 7.5 hours per day, with some women working upto 10 hours and more. This, work, though productive, is just not recognised. In the unorganised sector women almost universally get lower wages than men. In the organised sector almost 90 per cent or more are engaged in unskilled or semi-skilled jobs and on that pretext are paid lower wages.

As far as employment rates they are higher for women than for men. It is also found that under employment is also higher amongst women compared to men. The estimated back log of unemployment among women in the year 1990 was 3.96 million. There are about 30 per cent rural households headed by women who bear all the burden of earning and caring for the families and suffer on account of lack of access to land and other property. Yet, the trend of increase in the incidence of open unemployment is stronger in the case of women than men.

It has also been observed that processes of modernisation and economic liberalisation have affected the job opportunities for women. These on the one hand have reduced the jobs and on the other have created necessity of technical and skill qualifications for various jobs which are just not available to most women, more in rural areas.

(4) Social Indicators. The Indian Constitution guarantees legal and social equality to women. There had also been enacted various laws to make the equality in fact. Yet if a close scrutiny of the existing legislation is made, it would be abundantly clear that in social sphere the rights of women are still inferior to those of men. What is more important in practice social behaviour towards women in full of biases.

The old notions of Hindu law of inheritance which discriminate against women, still persist. Only in November 1995 Supreme Court has given a new interpretation to these laws which strengthens the position of women. The Matrimonial law in India varies with every community, there being no uniform civil code. Religion based personal laws in almost all the communities are discriminatory against women in one form or other.

At social behaviour level the attitude and outlook towards women's place and role in society remains almost medieval. The rising incidence of crime and violence against women are manifestations of a deep rooted social malaise and an expansion of a gender ideology which systematically discriminates and oppresses women. The challenges posed by cultural, caste, ethnic, religious and revivalist forces are part of today's social and political reality jeopardising women's right to survival with dignity. Threat and/or use of violence against women has been increasing over the years despite legislative enactments. There is a rising trend in reported rape cases against Scheduled Castes and Scheduled Tribes women. Problems of escalating dowry and violence against women negate the gains from women's participation in the freedom struggle.

The wave of fundamentalist xenophobic upsurges sweeping ·across the world is also threatening the women's movement as a whole. In India, these have adopted aggressive postures, showing scant regard for the Indian Constitution or the fundamental rights its guarantees. All religious, ethnic or cultural fundamentalists are basically hostile to gender equality whatever the rhetoric they profess. Indu Agnihotri and Venna Muzumdar point out that the fundamentalist/communalist organisations, aware of the ferment in women's minds, are today making a bid to chanelise/harness, the nascent consciousness about women's rights for their own purpose.

Taking advantage of women's deep attachment to religion they are today floating new organisations and fronts such as the Hindu Mahila Sammelan and the Durga Vahini, wherein women's role as mothers, progenitors and defenders of the faith etc. are highlighted along with their role in the family.

In matters of property inspite of recent laws and judicial decisions giving women's equal share in the family property very often justice is denied to women by their families. In many instances, the women concerned are illiterate and, therefore, are duped into signing away their legal rights to property. If they are aware of their rights, they are either coerced or emotionally blackmailed into giving up their share in the interests of maintaining harmonious relations with their families. Women are also hampered in their quest for justice by the fact that necessary documents related to inherited land are either not available cr withheld from them by local administration or village panchyats.

Thus, in actual practice, inspite of visible improvement in conditions of women in various middle classes, and constitutional guarantees of equality and freedom, the oppression of women and their unequal status within the family continues. In fact, even in the case of middle class working women, employment has not really changed the role and status of women in India. It has only meant adding to the existing roles of women without a corresponding redefinition of the roles of other with whom they interact. The increasing use of birth control and the growth of the small family norm have helped in emancipating women somewhat in this strata though this trend is by no means unambiguous, for nuclear families have made child rearing more onerous and anxiety provoking for the young mother. Various women's organisation participating in the "Global Women's March 2000 Against Poverty and Violence" highlighted the following points were regard to women's position.

- Women to two-thirds of the work, earn one-third of the income, own one-hundredth of the property.
- Hundred per cent of women income goes for family survival as compared to partial contributions of male incomes.
- The percentage of women has never crossed 10 per cent in the Lok Sabha or in State Assemblies. The affirmative action to rectify this in the shape of the Women's Reservation Bill is still pending.
- Violence against women and children is growing as minor girls constitute almost thirty per cent of all victims of sexual assault cases. Conviction rates are below ten per cent in all cases of atrocities against women.
- Female illiteracy is one-third more than male illiteracy. Girl drop-out rates are higher.

As already mentioned, in the twentieth century there had been growing a consistent concern about the women's status and gender justice. One important aspect of this during that period had been emergence of women's studies. These studies have tried to locate the causes for the existing status of women and failures in developmental programmes. The Government of India setup a Committee on the Status of Women (CSW) in 1971. This committee in its report offered some explanations for regressions from the norms of development. Many researchers have also pointed out several reasons for that. Important of these are discussed below.

1. Socialisation. The process of socialisation both of male and female, children makes them grow with the future acceptance of their roles. According to Leela Dube the first importance aspect of socialisation of females in the family, is the preference shown to male children as the permanent members of the family and inheritors of the family name. Even if female children are given affection and made to feel wanted, the message is that daughter's stay in the paternal home is limited. The son is seen as a source of support and often in middle class households, strapped for resources, more is spont on the son's education. Girls are encouraged to play with dolls and house and kitchen games emphasising their nurturant and domestic role. Girls are also taught the notion of service of "sea"—eating left overs, withstanding pain and deprivation and developing tolerance and selfrestraint. Women are so trained for domestic work and repeatedly told that it represents the best that life can offer them that many of them become vigorous advocates of their home and family destiny.

2. Patriarchy. The notion of patriarchy was deep rooted in Indian society through religious commends. Patriarchal values and normative structure established more than two thousand years ago still persist though in a different garb. The hierarchical relations arising out of it are concentrated in the family. An illustration of the importance of the family as the social location of patriarchy in the Indian case is provided by the fact that while the political and economic emancipation of women was never opposed and in fact pursued as an important objective by the Indian national movement, efforts at emancipation in the family sphere were met with bitter opposition.

3. Lack of Funds. There has been an inadequate and lopsided investment in the social service sector of education, health and welfare services, the only development policies of which women were supposed to a target. Neglect of the critical issues of universal elementary education, universal preventive health care and adequate outreach of welfare services had left women as the major victims of planned development. In the process of structural changes as part of globalisation. social order expenditures by government are being further cut. This effects women more.

4. Biased Planning. Urban middle class male bias of planners has lead to neglect of or exclusion of women from the scope of policies and programmes for agricultural, industrial and economic development.

5. Bureaucratic Apathy. The nature of bureaucracy and law enforcing agencies, especially policy continue to be moulded in traditional social and colonial administrative framework. They are thus incapable to design or deliver appropriate programmes for development, especially at grass-roots level. In fact in implementing policies or taking action they express, though not always open, in-built bias against women's emancipation, more so empowerment.

The above shows that in the male dominated family structure, caste and kinship based society, lopsided development and planning designed and implemented by ruling mentality bureaucracy and inadequate resource allocation, the change of treatment of women has been quite inadequate. This non-fulfilment of expectations on the one hand and realisation of limitations of state action by itself has given rise to women's movement for assertion of their identity, acquisition of power and achievement of justice.

Women's Movements

It has already been pointed out that one of the striking developments of the 20th century in many parts of the world is the emergence of women's movement, wherein women have started raising their voice against inequality, patriarchal values and inequalitarian social structure.

In India the social reformers of the nineteenth century was the pioneers in raising discussion on women's issues like child marriage, prohibition of widow remarriage, Purdah, denial of education to women etc. The growth of nationalist movement, particularly the direction, strength and inspiration provided by Gandhiji created a space for women in public life. Combined with the social reform movement created a climate of acceptability for improving women's social status, while the nationalist movement provided an opportunity for women to take part in extra familial and non-caste activity and a new sense of power and self-image.

In terms of feminist movement Pandita Rama Bai, a great Sanskrit scholar can be said to be the founder. Author of the first book on feminism. "The High Caste Hindu Women" she was treated as a notorious outcaste since she married outside her caste. Rama Bai wrote and worked for the emancipation of women. She also established "Seva Sadan's" for women in prisons.

Quite a few women's organisation were started in 1880s. Many of them were dominated by benevolent men reformers and concentrated mainly on providing education and organised debate on social reform topics. With the formation of the All India Women's Conference (AIWC) in 1927, a new trend set up. A production of nationalist ferment, AIWC was inspired, formed and dominated by women. It began with a modest objective of promoting education for women and creating awareness about evil social customs. From the 1930s the AIWC talked in terms of equality between the sexes as a necessary condition of social development. It also played a very important role in creating a favourable climate for new social legislation. During the pre-independence phase various state-level and local organisations were also founded, some by different castes and communities.

A very important aspect of these women's organisations was that its leaders served as role models for women who wanted to take part in activities outside the home. Though women's organisations were not direct wings of political parties, some of the women were members of political parties and took part in political activities.

Women's Movements in Independent India

After independene there was a general expectation that the new government with national movements heritage will bring social justice. Introduction of planning and emphasis on development gave credit to this hope. Most of the women leaders got accommodation into official positions. Nation-building imperative took priority over other debates. All this, to begin with led to fragmentation of women's movement and women's question faded from the public arena. The mainstream women's organisations got engaged in cultural activities, craft classes, beauty shows and philanthropic progranmtes. However, left parties were organising the poor women. They particularly in 1960s, participating actively in anti-price rise movements, the trade union movement, the students movements and various peasant movements.

Soon these activist women started realising that there was a contradiction between their activism on general issues and their passivity in the face of subjugation as women, in both their personal and public life. Also there was growing awareness among a new generation of women that all was not well and Indian women, despite independence, the Constitution, some social and legal reforms, despite increased access to education for women of middle and upper income groups, despite the country's then woman-headed government. Thus in 1970s the women's movement started getting a new shape and rejuvenation. The year 1975, in particular gave impetus to this.

The year 1975 heralded two or three crucial events. It was in the early part of the year that the Committee on Status of Women in India (CSWI) presented a document entitled "Towards Equality" which pointed out some of the glaring inequalities and worsening position of women in Indian society. 1975 was the International Women's year, which was later extended to decade. The decade not only provided an opportunity for drawing attention to women's issues but it also stimulated the growth of new women's groups. Finally it was the year when the Indian Government declared an emergency, when for nearly two years, dissenting women's organisations were unable to function. It is worthwhile to remember that it was during this year for the first time, March 8th was celebrated us International Women's Day, when a huge united left conference of women of left scholars and activists in Trivendrum was convened. There were indications of a new style of women's organisations. During last two decades a number of new autonomous women's groups have emerged.

These groups and organisations provide an alternate pattern of working for women's course. In contrast to earlier, established women's organisations the new groups are ready to protest militantly against injustice in the streets if need be. There autonomous groups have taken up a wide range of issues: rape, alcoholism linked of wife beatings, dowry, violence in the family, the problems of working women, traffic in women, devadasi system, superstition and witch hunting, the torture and harassment of women undertrials and prisoners, women's health, personal laws, the socio-economic and cultural oppression of tribal women.

Of course there are differences in women's group both in terms of ideology and interest and style of functioning. On the basis of ideology the movements and organisations can be said to representing liberal Feminism, Radical Feminism and Socialist Feminism. In terms of interests and style of functioning women's organisations according to Neera Desai can be divided into six categories.

1. Agitational propagandist, consciousness raising groups which may be termed autonomous groups.

2. Grass-roots or mass based organisations like trade unions, agricultural labours organisations, democratic rights groups, tribal organisations etc.

3. Groups involved in research and documentation on women's issues wherein both academics and activists are members of these groups.

4. Groups that concentrate on providing services, shelter homes etc. to needy women.

5. Women's wings or fronts of the political parties.

6. Professional women's organisations such as doctors, lawyers, scientists, researchers, journalists etc. that seek to agitate against discrimination more often create alternate channels for professional activity.

●●●

3

Women and World

The change in the status of women in India is a slow, steady and continuing process. It began a century and half ago when Rammohan Roy and his successors and followers focussed attention on the social evils which victimised women and thereby hampered progress. The founding of the Brahmo Samaj in 1828 started the movement for the emancipation of Indian women from the clutches of ignorance and evil social customs. Two developmental trends run through the movement for reform and change, which are interesting. The reform movement led by the Brahmo Samaj and continued by a host of others wanted to eliminate evils, which not only hampered progress but also enslaved women to harsh customs.

It was a humanitarian and rational movement and led to the abolition of suttee and the validation of widow remarriage by legislation. The initiative came from the people and it was supported by enlightened administrators like Lord William Bentinick who responded to the call for action promptly. The revivalist group like the Arya Samaj also initiated reform and encouraged girl's education. But they found their raison d'etre in the ancient past when women were free and not bound down by the existing evils, and these later were regarded as a violation of the true traditions of India. The efforts of these two groups were supplemented by the attempts of the foreign Christian missionaries to open schools for girls. All these agencies played a significant role in changing the status of women in India.

Why only do we talk of equal status when our scriptures have already gone ahead by recognising the women as the sacred *Janani* (The mother). Quoting a proverb from the old Testament, we are told, "She looketh well to the ways of her household, and eateth not the bread of idleness." Similarly Guru Nanak has warned those who assign the 2nd place to women. "It is she who gives birth to the kings." In the Hindu scriptures, she is dubbed as *Devi* (Deity) and *Shakti* (Power) the most cherished symbol of love and creation. She is said to be the power, behind the plough, the force behind the machine and the creative inspiration for the poet and the artist. In fact, it is the woman who has been the pervasive urge behind the creation. After having installed the Devi on the highest pedestal of reverence, what went amiss? What was it which brought the downfall?

Although the Article 16 of our Constitution has recognised the right of equality for women in India, yet the findings of the National Report on Women, which was published by the Government of India under the title '*Towards Equality*' nearly 15 years ago, were very depressing and discouraging. However, one good thing, which the report did, was the creation of a stir on National level. The condition of the women in our country could be so hollow, this gave us a rude shock and set the nation a thinking. It was, perhaps, under this stress that the Government envisaged the National Perspective for Women highlighting the problem. This realisation once again installed the proverbial DEVI at the centre of the stage, with care and concern all around. This was not a meager achievement. Since then various schemes have been introduced in the spheres of technology, education, health and agriculture, concerning the problems of the women. As a common housewife, she manages the house, tends the fields, looks after the cattle, works in the factories, mans the industry and yet remains in the background.

She feels shy to claim the equal partnership with her counterpart. But does the fruit of her labour grant her the status she deserves? In a country which boasts of its glorious heritage, where woman has not only enjoyed the equal status but has been described in the scriptures more than the better half, it has become necessary today, for the Government to create special laws and enforce them rigorously to give the desired social and economic status to the women in India.

The status of women in India, is tagged to the peculiar set up of our society which divided in itself among the unequal halves—the rural population and the urban population. Majority of women live in the rural areas are illiterate.

Thus a huge mass of humanity is ignorant about their rights or status. They do not claim it because they are not aware of it. They are not aware of it, because they are not educated. Taking into consideration the participation of women in our offices and factories, the percentage is low compared to man. This means that their participation in various fields of activities need a special fillip. The Government of India under 20 point programme have taken pains to stress on the objectives in this respect. While laying down the fundamentals of this scheme, the National Perspective very aptly comments upon the sad state of affairs concerning the status of an average woman in India. It tells us that the majority of working women are over burdened and underpaid. This is a very significant observation, which leads to conclude that the women in India have no other choice but to accept the life of drudgery. A wedded wife is a bonded slave for all times to come. The uneducated, unskilled woman is exposed to exploitation and special provisions have to be made to safeguard her interests. As such the concern of the Govt. is highly justified and genuine. The problem has received special attention of our planners who have included this in the 20 point programme. As a welfare state, it becomes imperative for the Government to safeguard the fundamental rights of the women and make provisions in the law for upgradation of their status in order to establish equality in the distribution of work and wages. One wonders why the simple principle 'equal work; equal wages' is not adhered to? Years of prejudices have dubbed the woman as non-worker and to crown it all, comes, in the way, her own attitude towards her man.

Toady the law grants immense power to the women. She has the right or equal status in the social, cultural, economic, and political fields. But what was lacking, was the will at her own part of claim equality with the man. It was the world of her own disbelief and ignorance, which always kept her as the shadow of her man. As such the first step towards upgradation is to educate her and make her conscious of her position and status. Though education in India is free and compulsory, yet she is not able to permit her children, especially the girls, to attend the school. The irony of the situation is that in spite of the protection provided by the law, she remains unprotected.

It has often been said that woman is physically fragile and temperamentally unfit to do strenuous jobs involving hard labour. But it is not the physical incapacity, which has kept her in the background. It is the illiteracy and lack of facilities for the technical training. It has been noticed that in the fields of agriculture, fisheries, horiculture, forestry and household industries, women have been working side by—side with their male partners. This statement is correct as far as the rural sector is concerned. However, in the urban sector, they are comparatively at a disadvantage, because their services can be utilised only in the factories as unskilled manual labourers or as domestic servants in the private and unorganized sectors. Although in the cities a small percentage of educated woman is employed in the offices as Clerks, Receptionists and Telephone operators, yet the percentage of employment remains very low. As stated earlier illiteracy is the villain of piece. There is no denying of the fact that better education and vocational training will improve their potential and equip them for both wages and self-employment. The Central Social Welfare Boards has come out with a major programme of Socio-Economic Advancement for Women, which will help them in setting up training-cum-production centres. Many other voluntary social organizations have also come in the filed. A tirade against the social evils like dowry, bride-burning, child marriage and prostitution have been started.

Exploitation of women in any form is punishable under the law. Education and publicity alone make the people conscious of the problem. In order to enhance awareness and mass consciousness of the rights of women, a programme of educative publicity has been taken up. The media has been entrusted the task of educating people regarding various schemes launched under this programme. It goes without saying that employment potential of the trained women is comparatively better in the skilled labour sector. As such arrangements have also been made to impart vocational training to the needy women.

Besides, there are other schemes concerning education, maternity and child welfare, which are the part and parcel of the strategy adopted by the Welfare state. The progress of these programmes will be monitored regularly on periodic basis by the department of Women and Child Development. For working women, provisions of creches have been made, where they can leave their children during working hours. Special houses and hostels have been built where, the working women can stay. These institutions not only offer accommodation but provide relief and support during moral danger. They provide care to the needy during illness, offer help during hardship and look after their legal and medical problems. Some programmes envisaged by the Late Shri Rajiv Gandhi (Ex-Prime Minister of India), lays specific stress, on the equality of women. With a view to achieve the desired goal the scheme has been described as the road to the destination. Some of the important targets, which have received attention at all levels are:

1. Raising the status of women,
2. Highlighting the specific problems,
3. Creation of mass consciousness about the status of women,
4. Provision of training and facilities of employment,
5. Participation of women in the nation building activities, and
6. Creation of mass hysteria against dowry and social exploitation of women.

CHANGING STATUS IN MODERN WORLD

"All kinds of magic are out of date and done away with except in India where nothing changes in spite of the shiny top-scum stuff which people call civilisation." This rather exaggerated statement comes to my mind as I survey the field of development and the change in the status of women in India. There is a substratum of truth in the statement quoted above. A hundred and fifty years of social reform movement, and two decades of freedom have not stirred Indian society to its depths. A prime minister, a chief minister and a few ministers here and there may catch the eye of the world in wonder. But the fact remains that the vast majority of Indian women, shut away from the main stream of development for decades, is still unaffected by the changes ushered in by western education, the impact of western ideas, international efforts to change the status of women the promulgation of a constitution guaranteeing equality of status with men and the legislative enactments to change their status. Two decades are over since India became a sovereign nation. We have had four general elections based on adult franchise. Yet it is not unusual to hear occasionally reports of suttee, human sacrifice and the almost inhuman treatment meted out to the less privileged people and prevalence of social evils long declared penal offences under the law. Therefore, one is justified in doubting whether substantial progress in desirable directions, to the extent necessary to change the status of women, has been made.

General Historical Background

India is a living democracy and its survival will largely depend upon our capacity to shake off historical conceptions and traditional attitudes towards women who form more than half the population in some parts of the country. With the down of independence a change has taken place with regard to woman's place in Indian society. Social changes, especially in tradition-bound societies, are accelerated by political convulsions. The struggle for freedom was one such. Yet it will not be incorrect to say that the participation of women in the freedom movement by itself could not have speeded up the pace of change. The ground was already prepared by the reformers of earlier days. It was the uprooting and displacement of vast populations as a consequence of the political settlement, which made the change urgent and necessary. An uprooted population, whatever its antecedents can have little respect and even less regard for the traditional mode of life and its inhibitions, when its very life is threatened by forces beyond its control. Just as in Western countries wars and revolutions have been instrumental in changing women's status, because they give opportunity to women to demonstrate their competence and thus change the attitude of the male towards them. So also in India the social revolution came in the wake of Partition. The line of social reformers begins with Rammohan Roy and is strengthened by an array of distinguished names, men and women, and the most recent among them was none other than Gandhiji who was radical in his belief that there is no justice when large sections of the population, women and other underprivileged sections, are denied a fair deal. His call to women to participate in the struggle for freedom was calculated to demonstrate to the Indian men that given the opportunity there is nothing to prevent a woman from contributing her very best for the service of the country.

These social reformers—their names are legion—are responsible for the legislation to abolish *Sati*, validate widow remarriage, raise the age of consent, restrain child marriage and raise the legal age of marriage. In the pre-independence legislatures attempts were made from time to time to modify customary laws which deprived women the right to inheritance, to hold property, demand maintenance, etc., but piecemeal legislation did not go very far to do away with the anomalies and harsh injustices which had a accumulated over the years. It was left to free India to deal with these things in a rational way.

Social Status

The social status of women in any community is largely dependent on the culture and tradition of the community. We boast of an ancient culture and swear by values, which are indisputably admirable. But in actual practice there is a good deal of conservative reaction makes us look pretty small. Scriptures are quoted time and again to demonstrate that respect should be shown to women. However, the existence of inhuman social evils and the age-long efforts to eradicate them go to show that this is honoured more in the breach than in its observance. That a woman's primary responsibility is to her family has wide social acceptance all over the world. In a progressive society it is necessary to create a climate of opinion, which does not condemn her to a life of drudgery and stagnation but gives her the freedom to choose her part in the life of the nation. In India, besides the security, which a stable government and a democratic constitution assure to its citizens, there is need for legal sanction against social evils which hampered an still hamper women's progress. The demand for participation in civic and national affairs was accompanied by an even stronger demand for social reform.

The raising of the age of consent, the restraint on child marriages, suppression of immoral traffic, abolition of dowry and the changes in the Hindu law were all meant to raise woman's status in society. So are the changes in the law of inheritance, legislation for equal pay for equal work, and equality of opportunity for education and employment. There is now no need for women to have any inhibitions regarding their choice of vocation. While legislation has been helpful, real change can be brought about only by a revolution in our thinking. As long as there is widespread belief that a woman's place is in the home she will be restricted in her understanding as well as in her activities. In order to encourage her to play her legitimate role, legislation must be backed by a programme of education. Education is the catalytic agent for social change. We started with 12% literacy among women in the forties and even now it is above fifty percent. This means that the vast majority of women are unware of the benefits conferred on them by the constitution or by the reform of the laws meant to raise their status.

All the same we cannot ignore the rapid spread of girl's education and the impact it has on our outlook. 'What does a women do' is becoming a more frequent question than 'whose wife is she.' While in many developing countries rights conferred by the constitution have remained on paper, here in India a definite attempt is being made to enable women to participate in development plans and programmes. The realization that no progress can be made without awakening women to a sense of responsibility is remarkable. Economic development as well as political stability largely depend on social progress. A developing country like India cannot ignore its woman power. We need vast number of trained and skilled women for staffing our services, ushering in programems of social welfare, toning up administration and reducing the rate of our population growth. Resistance to Government-sponsored programmes comes from illiterate, custom-ridden, tradition-bound women who are denied educational opportunity.

The elections to the panchayats have proved that even illiterate women are taking up responsibility with confidence and performing their tasks with efficiency. With more education their efficiency and understanding will improve. Economic backwardness prevents them from taking advantage of the opportunity before them. Equality of opportunity in education and employment, inclusion of girls in all compulsory schemes, and increasing attention paid to girls education have all contributed to the slow change that is evident in the urban and semi-urban areas. The goal is still far away and the change is still on the surface and not in depth. One hopes that notwithstanding our economic hardships, the social status of women will lead us towards the vision of our sages that heaven lies at the feet of the mother and the gods desert the hearth where women are not honoured.

The importance of education of women cannot be overrated. Many of our welfare projects dry up on the desert sands of indifference and lack of motivation. Motivation can come only when people are educated to understand their needs and appreciate the efforts by government and society for changing their status.

Economic Status

Political equality is meaningless unless it is supported by opportunities for education and employment. Before independence there was discrimination against women in the matter of pay, women receiving always less than men. Nor was there equality of opportunity in employment. This lack of equality is seen primarily in the exclusion of women from certain departments. Women were debarred from appearing for civil service and other competitive examinations conducted by the government. Certain departments were also closed to them the Government of India Act of 1935 prescribed that a person shall not be disqualified by reason of sex from being appointed to any civil service or civil post under the Crown III India other than those specified by the general or special order made to that effect by the Governor-general, Governor of the province or the Secretary of State. The following services had been closed for women under rules made by the Government of India: the Indian civil, medical, forest, police, the audit and account services, the railways and aviation. There was no restriction for engineering and judicial services, but there was little encouragement either from the government or from the institutions connected with them.

Equal pay for equal work was unknown and in the liberal professions like teaching and medicine, the grade given to women was very much lower than that for men even when they had identical qualifications. What was worse was that women doctors and nurses were required to resign on marriage. This was continued for sometime after independence but the government was compelled to abandon it because it contravened the constitution. All these pre-independence restrictions regarding opportunities for employment has to be given up because the constitution is clear that there shall be no discrimination based on sex. The inequality of sexes is, however, more evident when we deal with the legal status of women in India.

Several attempts are made for creating provisions to make women economically viable units of the community through programmes providing training for self employment as well as establishing income generating units. Even then studies have shown that these attempts have not yielded the desired results. One therefore wonders as to why should they not yield results? If one analyzes these programmes for the way they are planned and executed one would find several loopholes which need to be cemented before one goes ahead with them anymore.

Of recent origin the programmes aiming at promoting women's participation in income earning are those under Integrated Rural Development Programme popularly referred to as IRDP. These are the programmes which primarily aim at poverty alleviation and catering to almost 50 per cent women identified from the families living below poverty line. IRDP mainly aims at creating assets and providing loans as well as subsidies for establishing a small unit of earning for these beneficiaries. Such help aims at providing opportunity to set up a unit of sell employment or income generation. The most common ventures undertaken by women are setting up of shops, namely grocery, pan, tea stalls and handcarts by vendors. Other home based units of income generation in rural areas are units of dairy (*i.e.* keeping milch animals) and poultry units. Most of these beneficiaries belong to labour class mainly farm labours or to the families of marginal farmers. Therefore, they need to work in their regular jobs till they are confidently established in their self employing income generating venture.

In other words this self-employing or income generating unit that they set up becomes a 'secondary' occupation and not a primary one. This is because of the risk involved in it. Therefore is one wants to encourage rural poor to undertake self employment and income generation, one needs to decrease the degree of risk involved in it. A viability study in a given geographical area regarding the success of self employing or income generation unit thus becomes a 'must'. The question, which arises then is, who conducts this viability study particularly for women beneficiaries of the given area? The women themselves? The Women's Voluntary Organisations?

The Academic Institutions? Or the Government Agencies? The answer is difficult but not impossible. In order to undertake such a viability study the researcher herself will have to be conversant with the life of women in a given area. Their role in economic participation will have to be studied in terms of contribution, supplementation, saver, decision-maker, distributor and consumer. Various roles played by women in the economic sphere in the family are 'age' and 'family stage' specific. Therefore the 'age' of the beneficiary as well as the 'family stage' in which she is likely to be, become the determinants of her extent of participation.

In general, the age of beneficiaries is found to be ranging from 15 to 45 years. This group can be systematically divided into three subgroups, namely those between 15 to 25, 26 to 35 and 36 to 45. If one analyses these groups one would be able to identify the family stages in which these women would be found. The family stages affect their roles in family decision making as well as economic participation. Thus it becomes inevitable to consider these factors for successful implementation of programmes. The age and family stage to which women belong affects their leisure time pattern in terms of its availability as well as utilization. The interests of women in these age groups and family stages tend to vary. Their ability to perform intrinsic tasks involved in a given trade providing self employment and income generating opportunities too becomes an important consideration for recommending or undertaking such ventures.

Education—mainly basic education and training related to trade is also an important aspect. The planners and policy makers assume that for a particular trade say for example tailoring and stitching of garments, girls possess basic skills. This assumption in itself could prove wrong if one analyses the curriculum at school level and the activities performed by girls at home.

On the other hand one also needs to explore the possible Scientific and Technological alternatives which are available for these beneficiaries for use to undertake and promote programmes for their utilisation in setting a self-employing and income generating venture. It would also necessitate the issues concerning identification of training needs in terms of targetted women for utilising these Scientific and Technological alternatives and viable methods of training for utilization of these units.

It may necessitate 'Training of Trainers' in appropriate methods of training and teaching the targetted population with varying degree of knowledge and abilities. The question which would again crop up is who should be trained, by whom and where? The selection of trainers rests with the local authorities and those selected training institutions often further select the trainers from closer areas to the venue of training. This two-tier selection too affects the qualification and qualities of trainers which are often found to dilute with the level at which one is required to work. There are physical constraints to this, which are very difficult to overcome. However, they are not impossible. Thus, what is needed is identification of trainers at grass-root levels and training them through individualised instructions or in small groups in units. The main problem indicated in this process is the 'economics' of such a training or what is known as 'cost effectiveness' of such training programmes. The general attitude of planners and policy makers towards such aspects is not very encouraging. They generally look for 'zero economics' rather than any amount of expenses towards it.

Low level of education and no specific requirement for minimum education level of beneficiaries further limit the participation of the women in various aspects of finance management beginning with project preparation, submission of project for loans and subsidies, filling up and routing necessary forms and then maintaining accounts. There is thus a need for guidance and consultative service centre as well as information centre. Such a service will be different for women than men and would require people conversant both with women from a given place as well as these procedures which are required to be followed for establishing self employing and income generating unit.

Looking to all the issues one may feel disheartened and give up the idea of promoting income generating programmes for women. It need not be so. What is needed in administrating the programmes with some flexibility in its administration.

A recently completed status study regarding Training of Rural Youth (Girls) from tribal and non-tribal blocks in Baroda district, indicated that though the selection of beneficiaries was done systematically, selection of trade for training was not done logically. Though the training institutions selected were of repute their selection of trainer or master craftsman was not good. Though the training in trade was done satisfactorily the management aspect for promoting self employment and income generation was altogether missing. Further probing revealed that the trainers in trades themselves had no knowledge about management aspects and did not know that the training imparted by them was for promotion of self employment and income generation among women. This was because each trainer treated his/her training independently and none of them were oriented to the philosophy and objective of TRYSEM under which they were employed.

Training of girls and women seemed to have been taken very lightly in various skill developing or upgrading programme. The 'kit', which is provided for Rs. 500/- was not defined at all. Even in the most popular trade *i.e.,* tailoring the 'kit' was not defined. Hence not provided to the trainees though provision for providing it was there.

Other venues like insdtutional management, food preservation and preservation units or construction and promotions of improved chulas, which could have been attempted at, under TRYSEM were not even touched. In hilly area like one from Jammu and Kashmir to Arunachal Pradesh there is enough scope for these income generating venture.

Tourism Industry, which has steady flow of tourists can help generate self-employment through:

- Utilisation of labour and services of people.
- Promotion of Homebased industries like handloom, handicrafts and cottage industries.
- Promotion of products like food products and decorative goods available through organised women's cooperatives.

A little economically better off women can establish self-employed units or enterprises and provide income earning opportunities for skilled as well as semi-skilled workers. The State Small Industries Development Corporation can identify female intensive traditional and non-traditional small industries and prepare a list of these industries. This list can be used for prioterising assistance—financial as well as experts—to the women who are interested in undertaking these industries.

The State Women's Economic Development Commission or Centre can boost the income generating ventures for women by providing training, guidance and assistance in:

- Studying project potentials,
- Developing projects,
- Submitting project for financial assistance,
- Giving loans and subsidies as well as,

- Supervising and monitoring these projects, and
- Preparing review and evaluation reports.

Such a body like the State Women's Economic Development Commission should encourage and promote programmes for utilisation of Science and Technology for income generation. Provision should be made to identify economically viable traditional and non-traditional trades for women. Opportunities should be provided for training women in skill upgradation and skill development as well as in management components for organising self-employing and income generating trades. Consultancy and guidance services be created for women in self employment and income generating ventures to clear issues and solve problems.

Self-employment and Income Generation from Women from Hilly Areas

Institutionalised Industries

- Extending meal services to motels, inns and hostels as well as tourist centres,
- Running motels and guest houses for tourists,
- Running fast food centres, Restaurants and Cafes,
- Working as guides for organized tours.

Animal Related Trades

- Raising Milch Animals and Dairying,
- Raising Sheep for wool,
- Preparing carpets, goblins and possible art pieces,
- Preparing articles from wools,
- Raising silkworms,

- Processing and producing silk, and
- Dyeing and printing of silk materials.

Forest Product Related Traders

- Identification and collection of medicinal plants,
- Bee keeping and honey production,
- Collection of forest products like gum and rubber,
- Extracting medicinal oils from plants like Nilgiri, Cloves etc.,
- Wood carving for furniture and furnishings,

Handicrafts Industries

- Preparing cane furnitures.
- Stitching traditional and modem garments from traditionally woven fabric,
- Preparing ornamental and jewellery articles,
- Preparing and decorating household artifacts,
- Preparing jam, jellies, squashes, sherbats from fruits as well as preserved food like pickles from animal products for ready sale in tourist areas.

Gender Status

Little difference exists between the sexes until the age for reproduction arrives; it is at this particular time, the time when the secondary sexual characters begin to assert themselves, that the preponderating superiority of the male is observed (Darwin). Although, according to this writer, variability denotes low organisation, and shows that the various organs of the body have not become specialised to perform their legitimate functions, it is owning to pugnacity, or perseverance and courage, characters correlated with the dependent upon these varying parts, that the male has ultimately become superior to the female.

As these qualities, which we are given to understand are the special inheritance of males, have been of such great importance in determining men's capacities and powers, too much care and pains cannot be expanded in analysing them and in endeavouring to gain a clear understanding of their origin. Sexual Selection, we are told, resembles artificial selection, save that the female takes the place of the human breeder. In other words, she represents the intelligent factor or cause in the operations involved. If this be true, if it is through her will, or through some agency or tendency latent in her constitution that Sexual Selection comes into play, then she is the primary cause of the very characters through which man's superiority over woman has been gained. As a stream may not rise higher than its source, or as the creature may not surpass its creator in excellence, it is difficult to understand the processes by which man, through Sexual Selection, has become superior to woman.

While the female has been performing the higher functions in the processes of reproduction, through her force of will, or through her power of choice, she has also been the directing and controlling agency in the development of those characters in the male through which, when the human species was reached, he was enabled to attain a limited degree of progress. Since the origin of secondary sexual characters is so clearly manifest, perhaps it will be well for us at this point to examine also their actual significance, that we may be enabled to note the foundation upon which the dogma of male superiority rests. Although the gay colouring of male birds and fishes has usually been regarded as an indication of their superiority over their somber-coloured mates, later investigations are proving that these pigments represent simply unspecialised material, and an effort of the system to cast out the waste products which have accumulated as a result of excessive ardor in courtship.

The same is true of combs, wattles, and other skin excrescences; they show a feverish condition of the skin in the over-excited males, whose temperature is usually much higher than is that of females. We are assured that the skin eruptions of male fishes at the spawning season "seem more pathological than decorative." In the processes of reproduction, the undeveloped atoms given off from each varying part are reproduced only in the male line. The beautiful colouring of male birds and fishes, and the various appendages acquired by males throughout the various orders below man, and which, so far as they themselves are concerned, serve no other useful purpose than to aid them in securing the favors of the females, have by the latter been turned to account in the processes of reproduction. The female made the male beautiful that she might endure his caresses. From the facts elaborated by our guides in this matter, it would seem that the female is the primary unit of creation, and that the male functions are simply supplemental or complementary.

Parthenogenesis among many of the lower forms of life would seem to favor this view. We are given to understand that under conditions favoring katabolism, the males among rotifera wear themselves out, under which conditions the females become katabolic enough to the without them.

So long as food is plentiful, the females continue to raise parthenogenetic offspring, but with the advent of hard times, when food is scarce or of a poor quality, the parthenogenetic series is interrupted by the appearance of males. Although, unaided by the male, the female of certain species is able to reproduce, he has never been able to propagate without her co-operation. Among the lower orders of animal life - notably insects we are assured that an excess of females denotes an excess of formative force, and that an excess of males indicates a deficiency on the part of the parents.

In the case of bees, the queen, which is the highest development, is produced only under the highest circumstances of nutrition, while the birth of the drone, which is the lowest result of propagation, is preceded by extremely low conditions. The working bee which, being an imperfect female, may not be impregnated, will, however, give birth to parthenogenetic offspring, such offspring always being male. In the case of aphides, the sex depends on the conditions of nutrition.

During the summer months while food is plentiful and nutritious, females are parthenogenetically produced, but with the return of autumn and the attendant scarcity of food, together with the low temperature, only males are brought forth. It is observed that in seasons in which food is abundant, cladocera and aphides lose the power to copulate; they nevertheless multiply parthenogenetically at a marvellous rate of increase, "giving birth to generation after generation of parthenogenetic females, so long as the environment remains favorable, but giving birth, as soon as the conditions of life become less favorable, to males and to females which require fertilization." We are assured also that if caterpillars are shut up and starved before entering the chrysalis stage, the butterflies, which make their appearance are males, while the highly nourished caterpillars are sure to come out females. In the case of moths innutritious food produces only males. Experiments show that when tadpoles are left to themselves the average number of females is about fifty-seven in the hundred, but that under favorable conditions the percentage of females is greatly increased.

The following is the result of one series of observations by Yung. In the first brood, by feeding one set with beef, the percentage of females was raised from fifty-four to seventyeight; in the second, with fish, the percentage rose from sixty-one to eight-one, while in the third set, when the nutritious flesh of frogs was supplied, only eight males were produced to ninety-two females. It is stated that although scarcity of food is an important factor in determining the appearance of males, temperature also plays an important part in their production. Kurg having found a few males in mid-summer in pools, which were nearly dried up, was induced to attempt their artificial production.

We are told that he was so successful that "he obtained the males of forty species, in all of which the males had previously been unknown." He proved that "any unfavourable change in the water causes the production of males, which appear as it dries up, as its chemical constitution changes, when it acquires an unfavourable temperature, or, in general, when there is a decrease in prosperity." From which observations, and many others quoted from During, Professor Brooks concludes that, "among animals and plants, as well as in mankind, a favorable environment causes an excess of female births, and an unfavorable environment an excess of male births." According to Rolph, also, the percentage of females increases with the increase of favourable conditions of temperature and food.

Among insects, the males appear first, thus showing that less time is required to develop them from the larval state. Of this Mr. Darwin says: "Throughout the great class of insects the males almost always are the first to emerge from the pupal state, so that they generally abound for a time before any females can be seen."

Recent observations show that among the human species nutrition plays a significant part in determining sex. Statistics prove that in towns and in well-to-do families there is a preponderance of girls, while in the country, and among the poor, more boys are born; also, that immediately following epidemics, wars, and famines, there is an excess of males births. On examination, it was found that in Saxony "the ratio of boy-births rose and fell with the price of food, and that the variation was most marked in the country."

That the female represents a higher development than the male is proved throughout all the various departments of nature. Among plants, staminate flowers open before pistillate, and are much more abundant, and less differentiated from the leaves, showing that they are less developed, and that slighter effort, a less expenditure of force, is necessary to form the male than the female. A male flower represents an intermediate stage between a leaf and a perfect, or we might say, a female flower, and the germ, which produces the male would, in a higher stage, produce the female. To this Mr. Meehan adds: "And this is indeed a natural consequence, for, as vitality exists so much longer in the female than the male flowers, which generally die when the pollen has matured, it is essential that they should have every advantage in this respect."

The most perfect and vigorous specimens of cuniferous trees are of the female kind. We are told that in its highest and most luxurious stage the larch bears only female blossoms, but that so soon as its vigor is lost male flowers appear, after which death soon ensues.

In the Evolution of Sex, by Geddes and Thomson, is the following:

> "In phraseology, which will presently become more intelligible and concrete, the males live at a loss, are more katabolic—disruptive changes tending to preponderate in the sum of changes in their living matter or protoplasm. The females, on the other hand, live at a profit, are more anabolic, constructive processes predominating in their life, whence indeed the capacity of bearing offspring."

Among the lower orders of animals, there appears an excess of males, and among the higher forms of life, man included, the fact that the male is the result of the cruder, less developed germ, has been clearly shown, not alone by the facts brought forward by Mr. Darwin, but by those enunciated by all reliable writers on this subject. As a result of the excessive eagerness in males, and the consequent expenditure of vital force among the lower orders of life to find the female and secure her favors, they are generally smaller in size, with a higher body temperature and shorter life. Among the higher orders, the human species for instance, although man is larger than woman, he is still shorter lived, has less endurance, is more predisposed to organic diseases, and is more given to reversion to former types, facts which show that his greater size is not the result of higher development.

Doubtless man's greater size (a modification which has been acquired through Sexual Selection) has been of considerable value to him in the struggle of existence to which he has been subjected, but the indications are already strong that after a certain stage of progress has been reached, even this modification of structure will prove useless, if not an actual hindrance to him. On mechanical principles, every increase of size requires more than a corresponding increase of strength and endurance to balance the activities and carry on the vital processes, yet such have been the conditions of man's development, that his excess of strength does not compensate for his greater size and weight, while his powers of endurance fall below those of women.

We are informed by Mr. Darwin that by a vast number of measurements taken of various parts of the human body in different races, during his Novara Expedition, it was found that the men in almost every case presented a greater range of variations than women, and, as Mr. Wood has carefully attended to the variations of the muscles of man, Mr. Darwin quotes from him that "the greatest number of abnormalities in each subject is found in males." He adduces also the testimony of several others who have practically investigated this subject, all of whom agree in their statements that variations in the muscles are more frequent in males than in females. These variations usually consist in a reversion to lower types—a reversion in which muscles proper to lower forms of life make their appearance.

In an examination of forty males subjects, there was in nineteen of them a rudimentary muscle found which is designated as the ischio-public, and in three others of the forty was observed a ligament which represents this muscle; but, in an examination by the same person of thirty female subjects, in only two of them was this muscle developed on both sides, whilst in three others the rudimentary ligament was present. Thus while we observe that about fifty-five per cent of the males examined were possessed of muscles proper to lower orders, in only about seventeen per cent of the females under observation, did this reversion appear. In a single male subject, seven muscular variations proper to apes were indicated. According to the testimony of those who have made a study of the various abnormalities in the human organization, the ears of men present a greater range of variations than do those of women, and the cases in which supernumerary digits appear in males are as two to one, compared with females presenting the same structural defect.

Of one hundred and fifty-two cases of this kind tabulated by Burt Wilder, eighty-six were males and thirty-nine females, the sex of the remaining twenty-seven being unknown. Mr. Darwin wishes us to remember, however, that, "women would more frequently endeavour to conceal a deformity of this kind than men." Although it is quite natural for women to abhor abnormalities and deformities, it is to be doubted if they would succeed for any considerable length of time in concealing the deformity of an organ which, like the hand, is usually uncovered and which, in waking hours, is in almost constant use.

One of the principal characters which distinguishes the human animal from the lower orders is the absence of a natural covering for the skin. That mankind have descended from hair-covered progenitors is the inevitable conclusion of all those who accept the theory of the evolution of species, the straggling hairs which are scattered over the body of man being the rudiments of a uniform hairy coat which enveloped his ancestors. We are told that a hairy covering for the body, pointed ears which were capable of movement, and a tail provided with the proper muscles, were among the undoubted characters of the anteceoents of the human race. In addition to these, among the males were developed great canine teeth, which were used as weapons against their rivals.

As the lack of a hairy coat for the body constitutes one of the principal characteristics which distinguishes man from the lower animals, it would seem that a knowledge of the order of time in which the two sexes became divested of their natural covering would serve as a hint to indicate their relative stages of development. In a paper read not long ago at a meeting of the Anthropological Institute in London, Miss Bird (Mrs. Bishop) the well-known traveller, gave a description of the Ainos a race of people found chiefly in the island of Yesso, and who, it is thought probable, were the original inhabitants of Japan. The peculiarity of this people is, that the men are covered with a thick coat of black hair. The women, we are told, "are not hairy like the men~" but "have soft brown skins." Union this subject of hairiness, Mr. Darwin says: "As the body in woman is less hairy than in man, and. as this character is common to all races, we may conclude that it was our female semi-human ancestors who were first divested of hair, and that this occurred at an extremely remote period before the several races had diverged from a common stock." After our female ancestors had acquired the new character, nudity, they must have transmitted it to their own sex, and by continually selecting their mates from among the least hairy, in process of time males too would become divested of their animal covering. Whether or not our semi-human anoestors were subjected to the scorching heat of the torrid zone, nudity must have been better suited to their improved condition, not wholly, however, because of its greater beauty and comfort, but because it was a condition better suited to cleanliness; and, as the hairy coat had become a useless appendage, or was not necessary to their changed conditions, it disappeard from the body of females, while doubtless for ages it was retained upon the body of males.

Idiots, who, by the way, are more numerous among males than among females, are frequently covered with hair, and by the acquirement of other characters more often revert to lower animal types. Mr. Darwin assures us that around sores of long standing stiff hairs are liable to appear, thus showing that hair on the body is indicative of undeveloped tissues and low constitutional conditions. The same writer, however, does not neglect to inform us that the loss of man's hairy covering was rather an injury to him than otherwise; but whether or not the diminution in the quality of prehension in his toes, the loss of his canines, and the disappearance of his tail have likewise proved detrimental to him, Mr. Darwin fails to state.

The fact that throughout the vertebrate kingdom males possess rudiments of the various parts appertaining to the reproductive system which properly belong to females, is regarded as evidence that some remote progenitor of this kingdom must have been hermaphrodite, or androgynous, especially as it has been ascertained that at a very early embryonic period both sexes possess true male and female glands. As high in the scale of life as the mammalian class, males are said to possess rudiments of a uterus, while at the same time mammary glands are plainly manifest; which fact would seem to show that in the high state of development indicated by this great class, male organs have not through the processes of differentiation become specialised for the performance of their legitimate functions. In reference to the subject of atavism Mr. Darwin cites as a case of reversion to a former type, an instance in which a man was the possessor of two pairs of mammae.

It is true that instances have been observed in which characters peculiar to males have been developed in females. This phenomenon, however, seldom appears among individuals of the higher orders, and among the lower forms of life where it occurs, it is always manifested under low circumstances of nutrition, or in cases of old age, disease, or loss of vitality. Instances are cited in which hens, after they have become old or diseased, have taken on characters peculiar to males.

In all "old-settled" countries women are in excess of men, and this is true, notwithstanding the fact that more boys are born than girls. Regarding the excess of male over female births, Mr. Darwin quotes from Prof. Faye, who says: "A still greater preponderance of males would be met with, if death struck both sexes in equal proportion in the womb and during birth. But the fact is, that for everyone hundred still-born females, we have in several countries from 134.6 to 144.9 still-born males... " During the first-four or five years of life, more male children die than female; for example, in England, during the first year, one hundred and twenty-six boys die for everyone hundred girls. In France the proportion is still more unfavorable to the males.

Although whenever throughout Mr. Darwin's Descent of Man he has been pleased to deal with the subject of structural variations, he has given us to understand that they are injurious to the constitution, and although he has shown that their appearance is much more frequent in men than in women, yet he does not seem to realise whither his admissions are leading him. He has proved by seemingly well-established facts that the female organizm is freer from imperfections than the male, and therefore that it is less liable to derangements; also, that being more highly specialised, it is less susceptible to injury under unfavorable conditions; yet, in attempting to explain the reason why so many more male than female infants succumb to the exigencies of birth, he expresses the opinion that the size of the body and "especially of the head" being greater in males, they would be "more liable to be injured during parturition."

Among the reasons urged by Mr. Darwin to account for the excess of women over men in all "old-settled" countries, is that of the exposure of grown men to various dangers, and their tendency to emigrate. Doubtless their is more emigration among men than among women, still men do not usually emigrate to a wilderness and rarely to sparsely settled countries. When men emigrate from one civilised country, they usually go to another civilised country; yet we are told that in all old settled countries women are in excess of men. While the dangers to which men are exposed because of their greater physical activity have been many, and the accidents liable to occur from their harder struggle from existence more numerous than those to which women have been subjected, still it would seem that the danger to female life, incident to the artificial relations of the sexes under out present semi-civilized conditions, is more than an offset for that to which men are liable.

The fact must be borne in mind, however, that the diseases and physical disabilities of women, at the present time, although dangerous to health and life, are not organic, and will therefore disappear as soon as through higher conditions they are allowed the free expression of their own will in matters pertaining to the sexual relation. As the diseases peculiar to the female constitution are not caused by structural defects, but, on the contrary, are due to the over stimulation of the animal instincts in her male mate, or, to the disparity between her stage of development and his, they have not materially injured her constitution not shortened her average duration of life, neither have they lessened her capacity for improvement.

With reference to the women of Greenland, Cranz says that while they "remain with their parents they are well off; but from twenty years of age till death, their life is one series of anxieties, wretchedness, and toil, yet, in spite of all their cares, toils, and vexations the women commonly ·arrive at a greater age than the men."

That the imperfections of the male organization are already beginning to interpose themselves between man and many of the occupations and activities of advancing civilization, is only too apparent. Sight, far more than any other sense, is the most intellectual, yet in the development of the visual organs it has been proved that men are especially deficient. Dr. Andrew Willson assures us that "Colour-blindness is a condition which is certainly capable of transmission to the progeny. In one family the males alone were affected through seven generations."

In an examination which was carried on a few years ago under the supervision of Dr. Jeffries, among the pupils of the Boston schools, in which were fourteen thousand four hundred and sixty-nine boys and young men, and thirteen thousand four hundred and fifty-eight girls and young women, it was found that about one male in every twenty-five was colourblind, while the same defect among the girls and young women was extremely rare, only 0.066 per cent of them being thus affected.

At a convention held in the city of Chicago not long ago for the purpose of organising an association for educational reform, the teacher of drawing in the St. Paul schools made a statement that "four per cent of all male pupils were colourblind, while only one-tenth of one per cent of female pupils were so affected." No explanation was offered for this strange fact, indeed, it was pronounced a mystery, "even oculists and surgeons having given it up as impenetrable."

That defective vision is beginning to interfere with the activities of men, is shown by the fact that in many instances, in later times, colour tests have been required to determine fitness of applicants for positions in various departments of commercial enterprise. In this country, during the last thirty years, much attention has been given to the subject of visual defects in seamen, railroadmen and other persons occupying positions of responsibility in which unimpaired vision is an important qualification. In response to a request sent by the German government through its minister to the Surgeon-General of the United States Army, for statistical and other information on the subject of colour-blindness, Mr. Charles E. Pugh, General Manager for the Pennsylvania Railroad, in September, 1884, sent to William Thomson, M.D., surgical expert for the same company. Of this report Dr. Thomson says: "The apparently small percentage of colour-blind in this table may be ascribed to the non-application of men who knew their deficiency, and to the fact that men in the service, knowing their defect, would leave the road before examination, and thus escape detection, and be enabled to gain employment on other roads where no examinations are required."

In several departments of the national government, attempts have been made to guard against the dangers resulting from imperfect sight. In the examination of recruits, the War Department at Washington, some years ago, issued orders that bits of coloured pasteboard, or "test cards" be used for determining the power of individuals to distinguish objects at a distance, while worsteds of various hues were employed to ascertain their ability to distinguish colour. In the Treasury and Naval departments were ordered similar examinations, in which the power to distinguish colour was a necessary qualification in the case of all persons seeking employment therein.

In the examinations ordered by navigation and railroad companies to protect themselves and the public against disaster resulting from imperfect vision in their employees, similar tests have been made. Among the requirements imposed by law, applying to engineers, brakemen, and firemen, in the State of Connecticut, are the following: "unobstructed visual field, normal visual accuteness, and freedom from colourblindness."

If Dr. Jeffries' investigation in the Boston Public Schools, and the report of the officers of the Pennsylvania Railroad, are to serve as a criterion in judging of the extent to which impaired vision is developed in men, or if among them one in every twenty-five is defective in the colour sense, the inference seems unavoidable that the proportion of them unfitted for railroad and steamboat service, for military duty, and for various important government positions, must be large. Hence, by these tests alone may be observed something of the extent to which, under the higher conditions which are approaching, the imperfect development in men of this one organ (the eye) may cripple their energies and check those activities which, in many instances, are best suited to their testes and inclinations.

Nor is this defective vision developed in men a peculiarity, which is confined within the limits of our own country. We are informed that in Europe, investigations analogous to those instituted in America have been followed by the same or similar results. Until a comparatively recent time this subject has received little or no attention, for the reason that the process of civilization and the various arts of life have not, hitherto, demanded a correct or highly developed colour sense; but with the requirements of more highly civilised conditions, in avocations demanding more diversified and complicated physical and mental activities, it is plain that man, because of this one organic imperfection, must labour under great and continuous disadvantages. Then add to defective vision his lack of physical endurance, his liability to various organic affections caused by structural defects, and his abnormal appetites which are constantly demanding for their gratification those things which are injurious to his mental and physical constitution, and we are enable to judge, to some extent, of the obstacles against which, in the struggle for existence, the future man will find himself obliged to contend.

Not only is man's sense of sight less perfectly developed than is woman's, but his sense of touch is less acute. The hand, directed as it is by the brain, is the most completely differentiated member of the human structure. It may almost be said of the hand, that it assists the brain in performing its functions. The female hand, however, is capable of delicate distinctions which the male has no means of determining. Although throughout the ascending scale of life, the female has been expending all her energy in the performance of her legitimate functions—functions which, as we have seen, are of a higher order than those performed by the male, through causes which will be discussed further on in these pages, within the later centuries of human existence, she has been temporarily overcome by the destructive or disruptive forces developed in the opposite sex-forces which are without the line of true development, and which through over stimulation and encouragement have overleaped the bounds of normal activity, and have therefore become disruptive and injurious.

During the past five thousand years, woman's reproductive functions have been turned into means of subsistence, and under the peculiar circumstances of her environment, her "struggle for existence" has involved physical processes far more disastrous to life and health than are those to which man has been subjected. Owing to the peculiar condition of woman's environment, there has been developed within her more delicate and sensitive organism an alarming degree of functional nervousness; yet, with the gradual broadening of her sphere of activity, and the greater exercise of personal rights, this tendency to nervous derangement is gradually becoming lessened. That there is reserve force in woman sufficient to overcome the evil results of the supremacy of passion during the last five thousand or six thousand years of human existence, from present indications seems more than likely. According to Mr. Maudsley, women "seldom suffer from general paralysis." We are told that this disease is frequently inherited, and that it is sometimes the result of alcoholic and other excesses.

Regarding the dangers to which women are exposed by excessive and useless maternity, Dr. Beard remarks: "The large number of cases of laceration at childbirth, and the prolonged and sometimes even, life-enduring illness resulting from them, are good reasons for the terror which the processes of parturition inspires in the minds of American women today." However, that the dangers incident to parturition, and the excessive nervousness which characterises civilised women, are not necessary adjuncts of civilization, but, on the contrary, are a result of the unchecked disruptive forces developed in man, and the consequent drain on the vital energies of woman, will be seen, so soon as through the cultivation of the higher faculties developed in and transmitted through females, the animal nature of males has finally been brought within its legitimate bounds.

4

Government and Women Development

The Indian Constitution guaranted equal rights for men and women but women did not get an equal share of attention or expenditures in government development programmes which adopted a welfare orientation toward women's issues. Since welfare expenditures were seen as non-productive, women's programmes were a low priority item in government budgets. In the name of Equality, documented that women were excluded from a large number of wage earning activities and that their employment situation was worsening as a by-product of the expansion of capitalism in India. In the rural areas there had been an increase in indebtedness and in the number of agricultural labourers. Women's employment in manufacturing and mining had declined.

Towards Equality drew attention to the large number of women working in the unorganised or is about which few studies at that time existed. During 1975 interdepartmental consultations were held by the Department of Social Welfare on strategies to improve the status of women. These consultations drew on the recommendations of the Committee on the Status of Women in India appointed in 1971 and the World Plan of Action adopted at the U.N. International Women's Year Conference at Mexico City. The Institute of Applied Manpower Research drafted a National Plan of Action for Women (NPAW) based on these consultations, and the NPAW was approved by Prime Minister Indira Gandhi and published by the Department of Social Welfare in 1977. A comparison of Towards Equality and NPAW shows the extent to which the perspectives of the policy-makers were affected by the CSWI.

In identifying the sources of women's oppression, NPAW directly quotes CSWI, "The impact of the transition to a modern economy has resulted in the exclusion of an increasing number of women from active participation in the productive process." In the area of employment, NPAW acknowledged its reliance on Towards Equality. Many CSWI recommendations were included: *e.g.* extending the coverage of the Maternity Benefits Act, providing more creches, paying equal wages to men and women, and setting up a Women's Cell in the Ministry of Labour. The NPAW did not, however, accept the CSWI call for a women's quota in industrial training programmes or a provision for women to re-enter government after a five year leave to raise a family.

Mrs. Indira Gandhi accepted the NPAW recommendations, but the implementation of the recommendations did not proceed smoothly. Government action on women's issues during the Emergency and the subsequent Janata Government was more appearance than reality. Nevertheless, women's economic issues had gained some government visibility by the 1980s. Since the submission of Towards Equality, one section of the women's movement has sought to shape national policy on women through elite political channels. In the summer of 1988 the economic problems of women received some national attention. Two important government sponsored reports, the draft National Perspective Plan for Women 1988-2000 A.D. and Shram Shakti, the Report of the National Commission on Self-employed Women were being circulated in New Delhi.

The Department of Women and Child Development of the Ministry of Human Resource Development appointed the National Commission on Self-employed Women, chaired by Ela Bhatt, on January, 5, 1987 and charged it with the task of conducting a comprehensive study of self-employed women workers and of suggesting measures to "remove constraints adversely affecting the interest of self-employed women." The National Commission decided to enalarge its scope of reference to include all women workers in the unorganised sector, and the government accepted this change. Sharm Shakti was signed in June 1988 and presented to the Government in early July.

Also in January 1987 the Department of Women and Child Development set up a core group chaired by Margaret Alva, Minister of State, to assist in drawing up the National Perspective Plan for Women 1988-2000 A.D. (NPPW), prepared by the Women's Division of the National Institute for Public Cooperation and Child Development. The draft NPPW was signed on February 20, 1988, and was discussed at the first meeting of the National Advisory Committee on women, chaired by the Prime Minister on May 17,1988.

Although the NPPW has a broader focus than Shram Shakti, they each implictly embody a distinctive approach towards the state's role in women's economic development: a technocratic institutional approach in the NPPW and an organisational-facilitator approach in Shram Shakti. The NPPW reviews the approaches taken toward women in the Five Year Plans and government women's programmes and the situation of women in various sectors such as rural development, employment and legislation, and it suggests "interlinked and coverging strategies toward a holistic development of women by 2000 A.D." Its recommendations include strengthening existing policies and setting up two types of institutions which coordinate women's economic programmes: Women's Development Corporations at the central and state levels and a National Training Institute for Women. It endorses a technically improved version of the existing top-down approach to women's development with new women-specific institutions to ensure women get their share of services. For example, the NPPW suggests that the Women's Development Corporations would play a major role in supplying women with credit.

Shram Shakti contains chapters that provide occupational profiles and labour force analyses of women workers, examine the impact of macro policies on unprotected women's labour, and discuss factors that impede and facilitate organising women. Its recommendations include expansion of existing labour legislation to cover various groups of workers and the creation of new procedures, offices and bodies to facilitate oranisations of women workers bringing complaints about wages and working conditions to the Government. For example, the report calls for separate Labour Commissioners for unorganised workers in each state, women's organisations and trade unions being vested with the right to bring complaints to labour court and the establishment of an Equal Opportunities Commission in the Central Government to investigate charges of discrimination. A certain amount of controversy surrounded these reports. Jaya Arunachalam, a member of the National Commission, attached a note of dissent to the report, criticising its quality and stating that most of the information in the report had already been covered by the draft NPPW. In turn several articles in the press criticised the politics of the NPPW's preparation and recommendations from a perspective sympathetic to the National Commission on Self-employed Women.

First, the mere existence of the reports reftects the acquisition by women of a degree of what Nirmala Banarjee (n.d.) calls "political visibility": "Government support is not necessarily based on worker bargaining strength, specific skills or the justice of claims, but.... [on] how far support to the group reflects favourably on the party's image." What facilitated the government making this connection were the successful organising efforts of groups such as the Self-Employed Women's Association (SEWA) of Ahmedabad led by Ela Bhatt and the Working Women's Forum of Madras led by Jaya Arunachalam. In recognition of her accomplishments, Ela Bhatt was nominated by the President of India to the Rajya Sabha and later appointed to the Planning Commission. The acquisition of even a limited degree of political visibility creates a relationship between women workers and the government. The government can use this relationship to co-opt the women's organisations, but the organisations' leaders can also use this relationship to influence the government. The controversies surrounding the NPPW and Shram Shakti represent contending approaches concerning the state and women, and they represent competition for power to shape the government's agenda in this area.

While these reports demonstrate that women's issues have attained visibility, they do not guarantee that new laws to regulate women's employment or new policies to assist self-employed women will be enacted. Like the enquiries established to study the problems of sweepers and domestic workers, these reports are only a potential first step toward policy-making. To what extent are women workers affected by existing labour laws? To what extent are self-employed women in the assisted by existing government development policies?

Labour Legislation

It is quite confusing to understand the variety of laws, which apply to workers, since many different laws apply, and many of the major definitions have been subject to much litigation expanding or changing the definitions. Enforcement is a central problem as Shram Shakti points out:

Factories Act 1948 Labour legislation in India developed during the colonial period. The first law, passed in 1881, sought to control the hours of work of children in the textile factories. Later laws covered women and finally all workers in factories. The passage of such legislation served to demarcate a formal from as is of employment. The use of labour legislation has been of limited use to these who are in the is. The first problem is the definition of factory, the site of work. The second is the nature of the employer-employee relationship.

The Factories Act, which deals with working hours, leave, health and safety conditions was enacted to regulate the conditions of work of only those who were working in a "factory," defined as that having a fixed percinct in which "manufacturing" work was being carried out. The Factories Act as it presently stands applies only to those units in which either 20 or more persons are working without the aid of power or where 10 or more persons are working with the aid of power. The act, therefore, excludes from its purview a vast majority of workers who either work in their homes or in units, which do not strictly fall within the definition of a "factory."

One consequence of the enactment of the Factories Act was that the employers in some industries found ingenious ways to avoid the applicability of the act to their units, by dividing their establishments into smaller units and giving workers work to do in their homes. In the best knows cases large bidi factories were shut down, and employers started issuing raw materials to workers who rolled the bidis at home and brought the final product to contractors. Since the workers were no longer applied to them.

Another obstacle in making the act applicable to all workers is the definition of worker: a person (employed directly or by or through any agency, including a contractor), with or without the knowledge of the principal employer, whether for remuneration or not) in any manufacturing process or in cleaning any part of the machinery or premises used for a manufacturing process or in any kind of work connected with the manufacturing process or the subject of the manufacturing process.

The provisions of the Factories Act were applied for the first time to home-based workers in State *v* Alisaheb Kashim Damboli (1954 8 FJR 494) and Ramchandra Prasad *v* State of Bihar (1956 11 FJR 96). In Modern Match Industries Ltd. (1956 ILLJ 335) persons were required to report for work everyday and were given a particular quantity of raw material to work on at their homes. They were required to finish the work at their homes within a stipulated period for which they were paid at a fixed rate at the end of each month. It was held that the persons were employed for hire, and as the employer exercised sufficient control over them, they must be held to be workers under the definition of the act.

However, before the Supreme Court, in Chintaman Rao *v* State of M.P. (1958, 14 FJR 103), a restricted interpretation was put on the definition of the term "worker" in section 2 (b) of the Factories Act. A person would not be considered an employee of another person without a master and servant relationship between the two. The question of whether a relationship of master and servant exists between an employee and employer has been the subject of judicial consideration in a number of cases such as Dharanpradha Chemical Works Ltd. *v* State of Maharashtra (1957 ILLJ 477), Birdichand Sharma *v* First Civil Judge, Nagpur (1961 AIR SC 644), and D.C. Dewan Mohideen Sahib and Sons and Anr. and United Bidi Worker's Union Salem (1964 2LLJ 633). The meaning of the above judgments is that as long as there is supervision or control over the details of the work, there is a relationship of master and servant. Since this constitutes a contract of employment between the two, the provision of the Factories

Act would apply to them. Thus it is not necessary that the worker works on the premises of the employer. Even if they were home workers as long as there was supervision and control over the work, the Factories Act could apply.

The landmark decision, Bhikusa Yamasa Kshatriya Pvt. Ltd. (1963 24 FJR 429), broadened the applicability of the Factories Act, stating that under section 85, power had been given to the state government under the act to decide with reference to local conditions whether it was desirable that the act should be made applicable to any establishment which was not covered by the definition of "factory' or to workers in a factory who were not entitled to the benefits of the act because of the definition of "employment." The difficulty, however, lay in the fact that the extension of the act was dependent on the notification being issued by the state government. The judgments after the 1960s broadened the interpretation of the definition of "worker." These cases were, however, primarily decided under the Industrial Disputes Act.

The enforcement authority under the Factories Act is the Chief Inspector and other inspectors appointed under the act who have the power to issue order to the factory owners. Any offenses under the Factories Act can be tried by the Magistrate's Court but only with the prior sanction of the factory inspector. Workers covered under the act can lodge a complaint with the factory inspector, but in the majority of such cases the factory inspector does not investigate or the employer is informed. A recent amendment to the act prohibits the factory inspector from disclosing any information given to him by the employee.

Shops and Establishments Act (1948)

Those units, which are not covered by the Factories Act are covered by state laws regulating the operation of shops and establishments. The Bombay Shops and Establishment

Act, 1948, applies in Maharashtra. The short title to the act states that it is an act to consolidate and amend the law relating to the regulation of condition of work and employment in shops, commercial establishments, residential hotels, restaurants, eating houses, theatres and other places of public amusement or entertainment and other establishments.

The term "other establishments" is a comprehensive term and includes such other establishment as the state government may add by notification in the official gazette and declare to be an establishment for the purpose of the act. Certain guidelines have been set as to what constitutes an "establishment," and they are as follows:

It must carry out business, trade or profession in an organised systematic and commercial manner. The intention to make profit is not an essential part of the legal definition of trade or business. The activity must systematically and habitually be undertaken for production or distribution of goods or for rendering material services to the community. There must be co-operation between employer and employee. It is not necessary that there should be a fixed place or abode, premises or location from where business is carried out.

Under the act, a complaint can be lodged only by an inspector and with the previous sanction of an official such as the District Magistrate or the Deputy Commissioner of Labour. An amendment has been made to the act to allow an aggrieved person or a representative of a registered union to make a complaint without obtaining the sanction of the relevant authorities.

Industrial Dispute Act (1947)

While the Factories Act deals mainly with terms and conditions of service, the Industrial Disputes Act (1947) was enacted to provide for the investigation and settlement of workplace disputes. The two most litigated definitions under the act are "industry" and "workman". Because the definitions are vague, there are conflicting judgments as to whether workers are covered under the act. The wide scope of the definition of industry under the act has been the subject-matter of a number of judicial decisions, such as B.M. Bannerjee *v* P.R. Mukherjee (1953 ILLJ 195), Baroda Borough Municipality *v* Its Workmen (1957 ILLJ 8), Corporation of City of Nagpur *v* Its Employees (1960 ILLJ 523), State of Bombay *v* Hospital Mazdoor Sabha (1960 ILLJ 251), Cricket Club of India *v* Bombay Labour Union (1969 ILLJ 77), Bombay Panj Rapole *v* Its Workman (1971 ILLJ 393).

The confusion created by these decisions was resolved in the Bangalore Water Supply Case. The Bangalore Water Supply and Sewerage Board *v* A. Rajappa and Ors (1978 LIC S.C.) set out the dominant test criterion in order to determine what is an industry. These tests are: systematic activity organised by co-operation between employer and employee, and the production or distribution of material goods and services for the community. After the Bangalore Water Supply and Sewerage Board case, "industry" was broadly defined to include shops, hospitals, cooperative societies, professional offices, doctors, and lawyers. Thus a large number of workers who were not originally protected under the act were covered.

In a number of cases, including the Bangalore Water Supply case, domestic work was specifically excluded from the definition of industry. The reasoning given in the Bangalore Water Supply case was as follows:

> Domestic employment cannot be regarded as an "industry" because the employment of a domestic servant has no resemblance to trade, business or industry. Domestic servants have a calling or occupation but it cannot be said that their employment is an industry. Nor are the private householders employers

> who carryon an industry as contemplated by the Act. Further, there is no cooperation between capital and labour, which is necessary to constitute the industry. The domestic servant renders services purely of a personal nature.

By a similar judicial reasoning home-based workers and other industrial workers would equally be excluded.

Though the Factories Act recongises a worker who may not be directly employed by the principal employer, the definition of "workman' under the Industrial Disputes Act is much narrower. A workman under this act includes any person employed in industry to do any manual unskilled or skilled, technical, operational, clerical or supervisory work. Thus, unlike the Factories Act it was not clear by a reading of the definition whether a workman engaged through a contractor in connection with the work of the "industry" would also be considered a "workman." It was therefore left to the courts to interpret the definition of workman according to the facts and circumstances of each particular case.

The test that stood out was the right of the master to control the servant not only in what he did but also as to the manner in which he did his work. In Shivnanda Sharma *v* Punjab National Bank (1955 ILLJ 688) the question was whether the dismissed worker was an employee of the bank or of the "contract treasures." It was held that the direction and control of the worker was completely vested in the bank. If a master employs a number of persons to do a particular job, the employees thus appointed by the servants would be equally servants of the master. The case concluded that it was not correct to say that persons appointed and dismissed by an independent contractor can in no circumstances be the employees of the principal party.

Similar principles were set out in Kanpur Mill Mazdoor Union and Muir Mills Co. Ltd. (1955 ILLJ 537) on who can be considered a "deemed" employee. Though the employees in the case were recruited through a contractor, the details of their work were supervised by the mill and so they were considered employees of the mill. The decisive test was whether the management had some measure of control over and could regulate the action of the employee during the time he was engaged in doing the work. In K. Keshav Reddiar and his workers (1956 ILLJ 139) goldsmiths were employed by the gold merchant to prepare jewels as per specifications and within a fixed time. They were paid according to the number of jewels prepared by them. Control over the work of such goldsmiths was retained by the person employing them. Hence, they were considered his workmen under the Industrial Disputes Act. After the 1960s the courts broadened the definition of workman and held that the test of control was not in itself decisive, and other tests for determining the relationship of employer-employee were equally important particularly aspects relating to (1) ownership of tools (2) chances of profit (3) risk of loss.

Under the Industrial Disputes Act, complaints can be raised by the workman under the act in respect to dismissal, discharge, retrenchment, layoff, change in service conditions and lock outs or closures. However, these complaints cannot be directly raised before the courts. A complaint has to be first raised before the Government Labour Officer. Both the employer and employee are then called by the officer for discussions which can drag on for months. The Government Labour Officer has no power to ensure that the parties appear for the discussions. If negotiations fail, the complaint is then referred to a Conciliation Officer. In a majority of cases no settlement takes place. Then the Conciliation Officer submits a failure report to a government official who refers the matter to the relevant court. Once remanded to a labour court or industrial tribunal, a case can take upto four years or more. There is no scope for interim relief.

Contract Labour (Regulation and Abolition) Act, 1970

The objective of this act is to regulate employment of contract labour in certain establishments and to provide for its abolition in certain circumstances. It applies to every establishment in which 20 or more workmen are employed or were employed on any day of the preceding twelve months as contract labour and to every contractor who employs or employed 20 or more workmen under those conditions. This act could also to establishments or contractors employing less than 20 workers if the appropriate government issued a notification in the official gazette in this regard.

The provisions of this act do not apply to establishments in which work of only an intermittent or casual nature is performed. Discretion vests with the appropriate government to decide in consultation with the Central or State Board as to whether the work in question is of intermittent or casual nature. A contract worker is defined as one who is employed in or in connection with such work by or through a contractor with or without the knowledge of the principal employer. A contractor refers to a person who undertakes to produce a given result for the establishment other than a mere supply of goods to the establishment through contract labour or who supplies contract labour and includes a subcontractor.

The procedure for prohibiting contract labour in a particular establishment is complex and lengthy. A complaint must be made to the Commissioner of Labour who investigates whether contract labour engaged in the establishment should be prohibited. The guidelines used include (1) work carried out must be integral to the work of the industry, (2) work should be of a perennial nature, (3) work is ordinarily done by regular workmen working in the establishment, and (4) the establishment should be able to absorb full-time workers. Even if the commissioner decides that contract labour must be abolished, he cannot pass an order to that effect. The power to prohibit the employment of contract labour in any establishment lies solely with the appropriate government.

Relevance of Formal Sector Labour Legislation to the IS

To what extent can IS workers make use of these laws for the improvement of their working conditions? Despite the positive interpretation given by the courts to the definition of the employer-employee relationship, home based workers and contract workers have still not been able to enjoy the benefits of these acts. Judges are reluctant to touch the gray areas which would according to them open the flood gates to litigation if IS workers were to be covered by the various labour laws. In majority of cases of home-based work the employers normally operate behind the scene. The intermediaries or contractors play the dominant role. They directly employ the workers, the raw materials are furnished by them, and the work of the workers are supervised and/or controlled by them. The principal employer may never appear in the picture. Thus all or anyone of the tests as propounded by the court may not apply to home-based workers.

The jobs undertaken by the contractor from the principal employer are viewed as contracts of service, *i.e.* the employer gives the entire job to the contractor whose job it is to complete the work. An overall specification is given but the manner in which it is to be done has ultimately to be decided by the contractor. The workers engaged to do the work are thus not considered to be employees of the principal employers. The employer is able to escape the provisions of the law by engaging a number of contractors. A case in point is when a large public sector company engages a large number of contractors to do the jobs of stitching the napkins. The work is not done at the site, and the raw materials are not given by the public sector undertaking. The contractors are required to perform a particular jobs *i.e.* stitch a number of napkins in a specified manner. The contractors then give out the jobs to a number of workers who stitch the napkins at home. The raw materials are given by the contractors; it is they who supervise the work and pay the workers.

In the case of domestic workers, the work is looked upon as privatised. The home is not considered a factory, shop or establishment. The home owner is not considered to be a business owner. The work does not involve profit or loss. No commodities are produced. Hence the work of a domestic worker is looked upon as performing a "personal service." The home owner is entitled to pay any wage and no labour laws apply. The result is that working hours and payment of salary are totally arbitrary. There is no security of tenure and no terminal or retirement benefits.

Home-based workers can make use of the Industrial Disputes Act only if it can be shown that they are employees and that the place where they work is an "industry." In the case of domestic workers they are not considered as employees and the place that they work is not an "industry" as defined under the Industrial Disputes Act. In the case of private sweepers, only those working in a co-op. housing society are regarded as employees and then only if this society is considered as an "industry."

The majority of workers in India are outside the scope of most labour laws. The Government of India and state governments sought to improve the conditions of certain workers not covered by the laws discussed above by drafting specific acts including (1) Minimum Wages Act, (2) Bidi Workers Act and (3) Security Guards Scheme. We will briefly review these laws to see whether they could be extended to the groups under study or serve as a model for legislation for these groups.

The Minimum Wages Act, 1948

The Indian Parliament began to set minimum wages for low wage unorganised occupations in 1948. A list of trades for which the law would apply was drawn up in a schedule attached to the act. This schedule was not exhaustive, and governmental units were empowered to add occupations after providing notification. The Minimum Wages Act intended to ensure regular payment of minimum rates of wages without unauthorised deductions to vulnerable employees so that they would be able to make both ends meet. However, despite the policy of the legislature to include in the schedule those industries in which labour is being engaged on extremely low wages, a large number of unorganised labour are still not covered by the act. None of the occupations studied are covered. Furthermore the implementation of this act has been extremely ineffective.

Bidi and Cigar Workers (Conditions of Employment) Act 1966

Another way in which the Government has attempted to regulate employment is through enacting legislation for a specific occupation as in the case of the Bidi and Cigar Workers Act. This act redefined employer, employee, and site of production to cover the millions of bidi workers in India. As a result of wide scale exploitation of the workers a number of committees were constituted to go into the working conditions of bidi workers. Legislation was passed in several states, but the industry was highly mobile and moved to areas where regulations did not apply. To prevent this practice, a central law was passed in 1966. Employers challenged the law in the courts, but it was finally upheld in the Supreme Court in 1974.

The Bidi Act contains provisions providing for the regulation of the contract system of work, licensing of bidis, definition of industrial premises, and matters pertaining to health, hours of work, rest periods, overtime, and annual paid leave. After the enactment of the Factories Act, the large bidi factories split up into smaller units to evade this law. A similar situation arose after the enactment of the Bidi Act in 1966: the employers switched to homebased workers. Although the act specifically extends to home-based workers, the enforcement has not been satisfactory.

Employers have found ways to circumvent the extremely wide definitions of employer-employee in the act. Employers began to introduce intermediaries who were neither contractors not sub-contractors. The employers sold the intermediaries the raw materials and bought back the finished product. The bidi workers were made to buy all the raw materials from the intermediaries and then sell them the finished product. In this situation it was argued that a market transaction was involved and there was no question of an employer-employee relationship. Despite all the problems, the Bidi Act is one of the only examples where the state has tried to develop legislation on behalf of home-based workers. After the enactment of the Bidi Act, the test of control underwent drastic changes and was more broadly interpreted. It might be possible to amend this law to include other types of home-based workers.

Private Security Guards Board Scheme

One more way in which the Government has sought to regulate employment is through the creation of boards, which set up tripartite committees that consist of representatives from labour, employers and the state and that arbitrate disputes for that industry. Boards have been created for security guards, dock labour, and mathadi (head loader) workers. As a case study we will briefly describe the Security Guards Act.

The Private Security Guards (Regulation of Employment and Welfare) scheme came into existence in 1981. It is applicable to the State of Maharashtra. Before the act, about 250 agents and agencies were operating in Greater Bombay and Thane Districts, regularly supplying persons to work as security guards to various establishments. The object of the legislation was to eliminate the middlemen and to create a pool of security guards and to supply them to the establishments through a board constituted for that purpose. The Security Guards Act includes provisions extending the Workman's Compensation Act and the Payment of Wages Act to these workers.

However, under the act direct access to the courts for redress of grievances in forbidden. The act provides for an internal grievance procedure requiring the Chairman of the Board to hear the concerned parties. These administrative intermediaries normally pass orders in favour of the Board and the employer. Further, if services of a security guard are terminated, there are no immediate remedies. There have been many allegations of nepotism and corruption within the board. Those who are favoured are allotted work while others have to wait for days or weeks and when finally given work are sent to far off places.

At present none of the legislation discussed above applies to the five occupations under study: domestic workers, sweepers, subcontract workers, khanawalis and fisherwomen. The first-three groups are casual wage workers and the last two are family-based and self-employment occupations. Thus different laws are likely to be necessary to provide protection and assistance to these differently situated occupations.

For subcontract workers (home-based piece rate workers) there are several possibilities. First, the existing legislation regulating minimum wages and shops and establishments could be amended to bring most home-based workers into the purview of these laws. Those who advocate this strategy argue that it is the simplest option and would enable resources to be concentrated, on educating workers about their rights.

Others argue that there are so many problems with existing laws that a new law based entirely on the nature of the employer-employee relationship and of the work site for home-based workers would make it easier to win cases for those workers. This new law could be modeled on the Bidi Act. The National Commission on Self-employed Women recommended a third option for home-based workers: the setting up of Tripartite Boards modeled on the Private Security Guards Scheme described above. Shram Shakti gave several reasons for preferring tripartite boards to a protective act like the Bidi Act: a board would take over responsibility for both implementation and enforcement; it would do away with the necessity of establishing an employer-employee relationship; it would enable security of employment; and it would give home-based workers visibility.

Although sweepers and domestic workers are both casual wage workers; legal strategies for the two groups differ because of the different status of the employers in each case. In the case of sweepers in private buildings, it seems that once a private housing society is deemed an industry by the courts, then the existing labour laws will apply to them. Such an extension of the definition of industry is currently being argued in the courts. Domestic workers are one category, which do not fit into any extended definition of labour laws. Hence, there is essential agreement that a new law is necessary for them.

For the khanawalis and fisherfolk—as self-employed and family based workers— traditional labour legislation based on the concept of an employer-employee relationship does not apply. The needs of these groups of workers revolve around social insurance issues—means of compensation if these workers are injured, become sick, or die during their working years, health benefits, and old age pensions—and around issues of small business—raw material, capital, markets. The first set of issues have yet to be addressed in a comprehensive way for any of the five groups of workers studied. The second set of issues has been addressed by the government through its policies on cooperatives and in its credit programmes for the self-employed.

Government Enquiries and Reports

Another way that the government has addressed the needs of certain categories of workers has been to set up enquiries or commissions to study the problems facing these groups and issue reports making recommendations. The establishment of such bodies indicates that the groups under study have some visibility and that representatives of the government are aware of the conditions that these workers face. Concrete action may not emerge from the recommendations issued by such bodies. In fact similar recommendations issued by a series of commissions over time indicate a pattern of government inaction. We shall briefly describe the government enquiries into the conditions of sweepers and of domestic workers.

Sweepers. Under the rubric of abolishing untouchability, a series of state and central government committees have been appointed sipce independence to look into the problems of sweepers. The first committee, appointed by the Government of Bombay in 1949, and chaired by V.N. Barve, the Scavengers' Living Conditions Enquiry Committee, issued its report in 1952, and subsequent committees in Bombay and Maharashtra state included the Malkani committee in 1957, the Laud committee in 1973 and the Mehter committee in 1983 (Vivek, 1986). The Indian Government's Commissioner for Scheduled Castes and Scheduled Tribes issued annual reports, which included discussion of the living and working conditions of sweepers. The National Commission of Labour, appointed in 1966, constituted a Committee to Study the Working and Service Conditions of Sweepers and Scavengers chaired by B. Pandya (National Commission on Labour 1969).

All of the reports made similar recommendations concerning the working conditions, length of work day, wages, and benefits of sweepers, and the reports focused almost exclusively on sweepers employed by government bodies. Abolishing the practice of carrying "night soil" and providing uniforms and protective clothing for cleaning public toilets were prominent themes of the reports. The reports advocated incorporating sweepers as permanent government employees, extending to them the provident fund and employees state insurance benefits that applied to government workers, and offering members of the sweeper communities opportunities of upward mobility through education and employment. The reports revealed that progress in achieving these objectives was uneven across the various states and even across municipalities within states.

Domestic Workers. There are no central or state laws regulating domestic workers. However, there have been sporadic efforts in this direction. In 1959 the All India Domestic Workers Union approached the Prime Minister with demands for extending the Minimum Wages Act, the Shops and Establishment Act and the Industrial Disputes Act to domestic workers. That year a bill was introduced in Parliament providing for the registration of domestic workers and the regulation of hours, wages, and conditions of service, but it lapsed. Little more appears to have happened at the national level until the 1980s when several organisations raised issues. In 1980 the Catholic Bishop's Conference of India conducted a survey of domestic workers.

In response to lobbying efforts by the Gharelu Karamchari Association, New Delhi, demanding legal regulation of domestic service, the Labour Bureau, of the Union Ministry of Labour, did a study of domestic workers in Delhi and issued a report making recommendations regarding the sector in 1981. The report describes domestic service as an "ancient occupation" that "grew out of a feudal labour surplus migrating to the city" and notes that, "due to omission of domestic service from any labour law, their working condition and hours of work are not regulated at present" (Labour Bureau). During the course of the survey information was collected on the personal condition, wages, hours of work, housing, welfare and medical facilities, and attitudes toward trade unions.

Workers were also called upon to make suggestions, which they felt were most appropriate for their cause and improvement in their working and living conditions. The Labour Bureau's report found that "Most of these servants belong to economically and socially backward communities of the society. Being illiterate and ignorant, they are open to exploitation by the employers," and recommended that domestic workers should receive statutory protection against possible exploitation by their employers. The report suggested that the following areas should be considered for regulation by law: working hours, rest periods, leaves, wages, written contracts, protection against arbitrary dismissal, settlement of disputes, registration with a government agency for the placement of domestic workers. The report also suggested the establishment of a welfare fund, night school facilities, and housing for domestic workers. Government enquiries and commissions— concerning sweepers and domestic workers—have contributed visibility to the problems of these groups. However, the reports have a strong "welfare" orientation emphasising the disabilities of the groups and not their contributions as workers. The ensuing reports and recommendations have not necessarily led to laws or to laws addressing the needs of the entire group under consideration. Thus sweepers working for municipal governments have had their employment formalized, but those working in private buildings have not. There has been no legislation enacted to regulate domestic service.

Cooperatives

A cooperatives society can be defined as an association in which members voluntarily join together to promote their common economic interests and distribute their surplus among themselves in proportion to their contribution made for earning that surplus. Cooperatives were first introduced into India by the British during the early twentieth century for the purpose of providing credit to the peasants. From the beginning the state played a guiding role in the cooperative movement through the passage of central and provincial legislation. The Cooperative Credit Societies Acts of 1904 and 1912, and the Bombay Cooperative Credit Societies Act of 1925. By 1945-46 there were over 171,000 primary cooperative societies in India.

At the dawn of Independence the Indian Government continued the state supervision of cooperatives (guidance, audit, inspection, arbitration, iiquidation, training of personnel) begun during the colonial period and expanded the state role in providing financial resources to cooperatives. On the basis of the recommendations of numerous committees, in 1958 the state established the National Cooperative Development Corporation, a new institution through which the state channeled most of its financial assistance to cooperatives.

In the First Five Year Plan the Indian Government expressed a commitment to cooperatives as a major aspect of development policy. The Second Five Year Plan announced a commitment to a "socialistic pattern of society" with an enhanced state role in industrialisation and an increasing role for cooperatives in the private sector. During the latter part of the 1950s the Planning Commission and Prime Minister Nehru for a time endorsed the idea of farm cooperatives loosely based on the Chinese model, but this idea was abandoned in 1959 in the face of fierce opposition from Congress party leaders. Nevertheless the government commitment to expanding the reach of cooperatives and strengthening cooperatives continued although the emphasis was less on equality and more on efficiency by the beginning of the 1970s.

The Fourth Five Year Plan stated, "It is only when cooperative organisations embrace all activities from production, through credit, sale, supply, processing and storage to consumer stores and act as an integrated system that they can fully discharge their social and economic responsibilities." Government policy in the fishing industry sought from the early days in independence to encourage the 'formation of cooperatives and to channel financial assistance through cooperatives. This policy followed the recommendations of the Fish Sub-Committee of the Agricultural Policy Committee which had recommended that state aid be given to fishermen and that it be given largely through cooperatives, which should give financial assistance, sell fishing requisites at a fair price, and should undertake marketing functions. These recommendations, including that cooperatives should be grouped together under central societies, Central Cooperative Banks should provide the finance for working capital, and the state should provide funds for improved boats; cold storage and transport, were largely adopted by the state after Independence.

Thus state resources have been available since the 1940s to encourage the formation and growth of cooperatives in the fishing industry. This has not been the case in the other occupations under study. State resources have not necessarily resulted in economic improvement for the majority of fisher folk. Government policies toward fish cooperatives resulted in an increase in the number, membership, and share capital of these cooperatives. However, there were numerous complaints of corruption and mismanagement in the operation of cooperatives resulting in massive losses by cooperatives.

Mass Banking

In the first two decades after independence, Indian policy makers had assumed that planning would lead to economic development and the elimination of poverty. However, a sluggish growth rate, the persistence of widespread poverty, and the capacity of the formal sector to absorb only about 10 per cent of the labour force, led to rethinking among planners in the late 1960s. The objective of bank nationalisation (enacted in 1969 and expanded in 1980) was to reorient the banking system away from the prevailing pattern favouring affluent, urban and large scale borrowers and toward a new pattern favouring rural areas, backward regions and small scale borrowers. Banking was supposed to shed its elitist image and develop a populist orientation.

The Reserve Bank of India designated certain sectors of the economy as "Priority Sectors" including agriculture, small scale industry, small road and water transport, and retail trade. RBI directed the nationalised banks to disburse 40 per cent of their advances to priority sectors by 1985. Government officials justify bank nationalisation in terms of its social objectives. They use the term "Weaker Sections" to refer to the disadvantaged groups —small farmers, landless labourers and artisans in the rural areas and petty producers and traders in the urban areas—whom the banks are now supposed to reach. These social goals are shaped by an economic perspective, that stresses self-employment in the as a means of generating employment to reduce poverty and achieve economic development. The role of institutional credit is seen as two-fold: *(1)* Removing the constraint of a lack of credit availability in the growth of small production activities, and *(2)* In cases where the small producers are dependent on non-institutional credit (money lenders, friends, relatives, merchants) substituting institutional for non-institutional credit.

The central bank lending policy to the poor is the Differential Rate of Interest (DRI) scheme under which banks lend at the concessional rate of 4 percent. DRI falls within the priority sectors advances. To be eligible for a DRI loan a person must have a family income of Rs. 3000 or less in urban areas or Rs. 2000 or less in rural or semiurban areas. The limits for DRI loans are set at Rs. 50000 for fixed assets and Rs. 15,000 for working capital.

DRI was initiated in 1972. Banks were first asked to implement DRI in certain backward districts. In 1977, under the Janata regime DRI was extended to the entire country. Initially the DRI target was 0.5 percent of the previous year's advances, and the target was later raised to 1 percent. DRI loans are advanced to people who are assetless; in theory no security is required. To protect banks from default by DRI and other small borrowers, the government provides insurance through a credit guarantee scheme. In the case of default, banks can recover 90 percent of the amount overdue from the Deposit Insurance and Credit Guarantee Corporation (DICGC) in the case of DRI and 75 percent in the case of other small borrowers. The number of loans advanced under DRI rose from 26,000 in 1972 to 2,253,000 in 1980.

The 6th Plan (1980-85) places special emphasis on unemployment and people below the poverty line. In 1980 an RBI working group recommended sub targets for priority sector advances designed to direct more credit to the weaker sections. Fifty percent of direct agricultural advances were to go to rural artisans and cottage industries. The government appears to be increasing its reliance on bank loans to the weaker sections as a strategy of economic development. The new 20 Point Programme announced in January, 1982 emphasised credit as an important component of programmes to reduce rural poverty such as the integrated rural development programme (IRDP). Increasing the access of Scheduled Caste and tribe (SC/ST) individuals to DRI and

Priority Sector advances is also stressed in recent government policies.

In 1986 another major programme was started in urban areas called SEPUP (Self-employed Programme for the Urban Poor). The rationale behind this was that for the rural areas there was a subsidy based programme (IRDP) but none for the urban areas with population over 10,000. So SEPUP was started with the government providing 25 percent of the advance as subsidy. The number of loans to be disbursed was 1 percent 300 of the population in the city and a lead bank was selected for each urban area or district to coordinate and target with the other banks in the city for the disbursement of loans. DRI differs from SEPUP in that the rate of interest in SEPUP is 12 per cent and there is a 25 per cent subsidy.

At first women received few loans under DRI, but through the efforts of several women's associations based among women IS workers—SEWA, Working Women's Forum, and Annapurna Mahila Mandal—women members of these associations obtained DRI loans. The khanawali workers in our study, members of Annapurna Mahila Mandal, had participated in these lending programmes. Few, if any, of the women studied in the other four occupations had gotten DRI loans.

●●●

5

Women and Development Process

Any in-depth examination of the integration of women in development as well as of their position and role in different sectors and areas of activity undoubtedly depends on an appropriate conceptual framework. In addition, an insight is needed into the institutional mechanisms that promote or prevent changes and transformations in individual sectors or areas of social and economic life. In this study the sectoral approach is used as an analytical device to illustrate the role and position of women in developing countries. It should, however, be kept in mind that the harmonisation of women's productive, reproductive and participatory roles cannot be achieved at the individual level. The inter-linkages among sectors and areas are therefore crucial when general development concepts are operationalised through development planning, development of human resources, employment, technological and scientific change etc.

The sectors and areas included here have been chosen because of their relevance for the advancement of women. Some relevant areas, such as employment, have been treated within all sectors. The measures proposed in relation to specific sectoral issues influence other sectors and institutions, and thus have a synergetic development effect. This is especially so in the case of science and technology. The transfer of technology from developed to developing countries influences the organisation of the production process in all economic sectors, and affects all other socio-economic spheres.

Agriculture and Rural Development

The current situation in developing countries in agriculture, food production and rural development derives from a historical pattern of development in which investment has been skewed in favour of industrialisation and urban areas with the result that in the majority of countries rural areas have lagged behind in their development. In Africa, Latin America, the Middle East and certain parts of Asia the development paradigms pursued so far have created food shortages and a structural cleavage in rural society.

The resultant rural transformation has led to a cleavage between commercial or large-scale agriculture, which has been rapidly modernised through application of scientific and technological innovations, higher capital investment with higher returns, and small scale subsistence agriculture with little or no capital investment and a low level of technology, requiring high labour inputs with low and even declining returns. Such developments in agriculture have sometimes been due to the need to earn foreign currency. Furthermore, this cleavage has taken the form of a gender differentiation in which men predominate in the decision-making and management of commercial or large-scale agriculture, while women continue to predominate in the food and subsistence sector in which they expend large amounts of labour—as evidenced by the long hours of work with low levels of technology and low returns. Moreover, within commercial agriculture the gender division is also reflected by the high demand for female labour in those cycle of production requiring hoe and hand methods (*e.g.*, weeding or paddy transplanting) with low remuneration. This cleavage has meant that many developing countries have not been able to attain the goal self-reliance in the areas of food, agriculture and rural development. A substantial number of countries continue to experience a severe decline in food production, leading to food shortages and even outright hunger and famine. Moreover, even in countries, which have been able to expand their food sectors, the system of distribution is inadequate and poverty, hunger and malnutrition still afflict large masses of the people.

According to the FAO, malnutrition and hunger increased by 15 percent during the seventies, affecting 450 million people in Asia, Africa and Latin America. In developing market economies as a whole, daily per capita calorie consumption has remained at 2 percent below the minimum requirement. The gap is largest in Africa, followed by South and South-East Asia. In Sub-Saharan Africa, the growth rate of agricultural production fell to 1.3 percent annum while population growth remained at 27 percent over the second development decade.

Women in developing countries are a major resource in agriculture, food production and rural development, as evidenced by their numerical proportions, their share of labour in agriculture and food production and the division of labour by sex in this sector. Their share of labour is particularly significant in view of the fact that in many cases they perform their agricultural work in addition to long and arduous work in child-care household maintenance, cooking and fuel wood collection, as well as food preparation and processing. Despite women's crucial role in agriculture and food production their potential for accelerating rural development has not often been well understood or appreciated. Inherited biases in the agrarian development approaches have led 'to an inadequate perception of women's economic role, undercounting or devaluation of their work and thus to a perpetuation of the dependency of developing countries on external factors of production.

The undercounting of women's work in rural economics results from:

(a) The use of industrialised countries definitions of work, employment, jobs, primary activity etc.

(b) The invisibility of many types of work in the subsistence mode of production, and

(c) The association of women's non-work with the family's social status in Asian and Latin American Countries.

In practice, women have not benefited from adequate policy support. First of all the accumulated evidence suggests that agrarian and land tenure policies have restricted women's access to land and other factors of agricultural production, such as technology, credit subsidy and inputs (*e.g.* fertilisers and seeds). Secondly, women have not had equal access to support services and incentive system for expanding agriculture, food production and rural development, for instance, extension and training services and information. Thirdly, lack of an integrated approach to development at the national level has consistently perpetuated a fragmentary approach to women's position in the society and their role in development, thereby perpetuating the promotion of women's programmes through social welfare, humanitarian and demographic approaches only, without provisions for long term integration.

In traditional societies women's role in agriculture and food production was recognised by customary rights of access to land, forests, and to support from family labour. Structural changes under colonialism and in the postcolonial phases have eroded many of these rights, but the responsibility of feeding the family still rests primarily with the women in many rural communities of Africa and in the economically least affluent sections of many Asian and Latin American societies. The privatisation of land and the introduction of cash crops for domestic and foreign markets, the need to feed expanding populations, and the depletion of forest resources for industrial and communications growth, which were initiated during colonialism and continued after independence, have steadly reduced women's access to basic resources. The withdrawal of male labour—for deployment in mining, roads and railway building, plantation of export crops and new industries—which was initiated by colonial regimes also increased women's burdens.

Despite international recognition of rural women's right to own land, attempts to incorporate this principle in land tenure and land development policies have been marginal. Forest policy, including policies for reforestation has yet to recognise the role of women in forest development, even though in some areas women have initiated major protest movement against deforestation, which have negatively affected their ability to feed their families and livestock. Case studies from Asia and Africa indicate that rural women are very dynamic and innovative in these fields when they are give the opportunity to participate collectively in such developmental activities. They also indicate a process of increasing self- confidence among women and an enhancement of their status within their families and the community. However, extension of such experiments to other areas will require uncorporation of women as a target group in policies and structures for agarian reform, and development of forests, agriculture, animal husbandry, silk production, fish culture, land development (including waste lands) etc.

Unless the structural constraints and the existing 'invisibility' of women in rural development policies and agrarian reform are removed, it is difficult to envisages an equitable growth and expansion of agriculture, food and forest production. It is important to take specific short-run measures to make them sensitive to women's potentials and the promotion of research and communication programmes for rural women in these areas. However, the solution to the problem lies in the establishment of long-term strategies and measures to implement them as a matter of national priority in the context of solutions to, for example chromic food problems deforestation and ecological imbalances, unemployment and poverty, and to enhance the process of corrective and individual self-reliance.

New initiatives are needed to reorient agricultural policies at the national level, which would give priority to a balanced approach to agricultural communities and food production. Within this policy restructuring process, a number of specific issues arise. A food strategy might be designed to support rural development and agrarian reforms and other relevant measures for strengthening and food sector recommended. Since food strategies are relatively new initiatives, whose policy guidelines are still being drawn up, they could provide an important policy intervention to strengthen women's role in food production.

In view of the role of women in farming and the inadequacy of access to services for expanding production the following measures could be fruitful:

— savings and investment programmes should aim at providing credit, finance and subsidies for women through various channels:

(a) regular agricultural financing institutions and credit programmes could include the elaboration of specific mechanisms for assisting farm women; and

(b) revolving funds and credit subsidies extended to women through their associations net-works, and local level groups, as well as government

offices at the local level, in conjunction with information campaigns to encourage women to use these services.

- new organisational schemes, especially those at the community level should be extended through women's groups and associations;
- current farmer training programmes, including the Technical Cooperation among Developing Countries (TCDC) programmes, could be reviewed and modified to cater for women farmers. An important elements of adjustment here would be to provide agricultural training programmes which would increase women's technical knowledge and allow them to combine mothering and training opportunities;
- increasing women's competence to participate in rural institutions, decision making and designs for agricultural and food programmes.

The persistence of the subordinate position of women in society, as illustrated by the experience in the agriculture and food sector, is a negation of the goals of development, which affects ill members of society equally, regardless of sex or creed.

Development Through Technology

In view of the importance of industrialisation, the pattern of industrial is at ion adopted in developing countries is most relevant. Differences in the socio-economic environment of individual developing countries resulted in various industrialisation strategies. However, regardless of the different industrialisation policies and practices of the individual developing countries, they have a common desire to generate national product, promote employment and secure the most dynamic possible modernisation, so as to secure a greater degree of technological and financial independence from the developed countries. The level and the features of the industrialisation of developing countries are usually determined by the individual country's resources, both material and human, and by its past experience of development.

The great dependence of the industrialisation processes in developing countries or developed countries, on technology transfer, capital investment, export. markets, etc., has resulted in a high degree of exploitation and in unbalanced industrial structures which are highly sensitive to international economic fluctuations. Thus, the introduction of new industries and changes. In the industrial structure of a developing country may profoundly and rapidly influence the overall economic structure. Such influences may bring about unexpected or unplanned changes and social life. Developing countries often find it difficult to fully control the structural changes in their industries and thus avoid industrial instability and exploitation of the workforce. This may to some extent be possible for those countries, which have large internal markets, strong public sectors, or were able to control investments in industrial development through generation of sufficient internal funds.

The share of women in industrial employment in developing countries rose from 21 percent to 26.5 percent in 1980. About two thirds of the net increase in the female industrial workforce (the number of women employed in industry in the world increased by 104 percent in the last two decades) took place in developing countries mainly in Asia. In contrast to Africa and Latin America, Asia has a higher share of the female than of the male world industrial labour force.

Women are usually engaged in labour-intensive industries with low productivity (*e.g.* processing industries—

textile, food, leather, etc.). Their wages are influenced by their poor bargining position, and they have no influence at all on working conditions. Thus, for instance, although the working hours in manufacturing have generally tended to decline, in some developing countries working hours have tended to rise. The treatment of the female labour force is to a large extent a reflection of women's low status on the labour market, lack of proper education and training low or non-existent organisation, the lack of or non-implementation of protective legislation (particularly in export-oriented industries) and their generally unfavourable social position. The recent upward trend in women's employment in developing countries is not very significant in relation to the absolute size of the female population or workforce in these countries. Moreover, although this increase is in some of the most modern industries in the world, it does not appear to have made a substantial difference to women status, since it has done little to break the isolation and discrimination of women in the industrial workforce. The extension of the practice of subcontracting of home workers for certain stages of industrial production processes may have considerable counter-productive consequences,. for women's formal employment. Such organisational changes may sometimes lead to a circumvention of legal protective measures for labour, a deterioration of working conditions, lower wages within and outside industry, greater exploitation of women's and children's labour, diminishing union activity and, in the long run, also to increased formal unemployment of both men and women. While the short-term positive effects of income generation cannot be discounted, the negative effects of channelling or restricting women's employment to the informal sector make it considerably more difficult and could lead to a higher degree of isolation, exploitation and inequality of women, by excluding them from the mainstream of socio-economic activity.

It is unlikely that the position of women in the industries of developing countries can be changed without changes in the models of industrial development and organisation of industrial production. Therefore, formulation and implementation of national industrialisation policies based on the needs and interests of all strata of the population, as well as on an evaluation of domestic potentials continue to be priority tasks confronting developing countries. The existing potentials of developing countries are certainly conducive to positive changes. Balanced development planning and policies which aim at maximum utilisation of national resources and at an expansion of domestic demand are also the proper framework for the advancement of the role of women in this sector of the economic and for promotion within overall development.

To improve women's position in industry, a number of measures would have to be incorporated in the industrial policies of developing countries:

- changes in education, which would enable women to improve their position in industrial employment, and to acquire transferable skills through various forms of vocational and informal training;
- legal arrangements covering all aspects of industrialisation, from investment codes to regulations, which would provide for better general treatment of labour in industry. In this connection, there should be regulatory measures in free exporting zones to ensure that social costs are also covered. However, it must be recognised that collective action by the developing countries is needed for the successful legislation and implementation of such measures;
- adoption of technologies which ensure stability of employment and professional progress to women workers;

- extention of employment opportunities in accordance with human resources development policies;
- establishment of overall social control and of schemes for genuine workers' participation in management and decision making;
- selection, development and transfer of technology and know-how as well as training of personnel;
- elaboration of criteria for determining the size of enterprises in various industrial branches and the ways of organising them; promotion of small and medium-size enterprises in developing countries; establishment of industrial cooperatives;
- strengthening of self-reliance in industrial policy through industrial cooperation among developing countries, exchange of information and experience through ECDC/TCDC programmes and projects.

This would improve the bargaining position of developing countries *vis-a-vis* developed ones, particularly in case of transfer of technology or foreign investment, in enforcement of national legal mechanisms for the protection of the industrial labour force, including women workers. All this calls for urgent action among developing countries in the field of industrialisation.

Technological Development

The main issue connected with the utilisation of science and technology as a pool to speed up the development of the developing countries is, therefore, the transfer of technology and, in this respect, the choice of technology. Technology being a system consisting of hardware and software the transfer of technology must be viewed as a complex process, involving a range of economic, financial, legal and sociological factors.

In this connection, local inputs-primarily knowledge and information on technologies, trained cadres, legal and other regulations, etc.—are needed. The process of selection of technologies calls for an analysis and assessment not only of the economic impact, but also of the social impact. While must be kept in mind is that while technology itself is natural, the application of technology can have considerable social effects, since, through technology, a system of domination and exploitation, as well as a set of social norms and ethics may be transferred. A social impact analysis should be a constituent part of any transfer of technology arrangement.

Women are involved in science and technology through the structural transformations that occur with the transfer of technology and scientific and technological development, and as participants in research and technological activities; and experiencing the impact of the technologies on their everyday lives. In all cases, their involvement should be much stronger than it is at present. It is also very important that women understand scientific and technological innovations, because this enables them to influence the general social attitudes towards technological change through the existing non-formal education. The radical changes in the organisational pattern and activities of the society, associated with rapid scientific and technological change in the overall organisation, which are presently being experienced in the developed countries, may also dramatically affect all developing countries, and lead to either a more dynamic and humane development or to an ever higher degree of dependency and exploitation. The problem of the marginal position of some members of society, and of women specifically, cannot be solved unless the elements of these new technologies can be built into development strategies in accordance with the concept of integral development. Furthermore, the latest so-called frontier and trans-disciplinary technologies can be used in different ways and at different levels. Their use can serve to accontuate the productive role of women, because such technologies are applicable to a number of areas which are of relevance to the betters quality of life and to the integration of women in development, *i.e.* food production, clean water supply, improved housing conditions, use of alternative energy sources, in the services education etc.

It should be kept in mind that it is economic and political considerations, rather than social and cultural ones, which determine the availability and terms and conditions for the access of developing countries to new technologies and which are important for national development. Women's access to technological development thus also depends on the global relations between the technology owners and users and those who try to secure access to new technology and to processes of industrialisation.

Women have traditionally gained knowledge and experience (*e.g.*, in agricultural production, energy utilisation, running the household, manufacturing objects for everyday use, home medicine etc.,), which have not been, exploited from the developmental point of view. The application of new scientific and technological devices and knowledge may lighten household drudgery in urban and rural areas, providing better water, energy and other community facilities. This would release energies which women might be encouraged to direct forwards active and useful participation in other economic and social areas, and in the overall technological transformation of the society.

A greater involvement of women in scientific and technological development would therefore require:

— popularisation of scientific and technological knowledge and skills in order to enable their further development, by mass media, through changes in school programmes, and through all participatory and community development activities (especially in agriculture but also in other areas, *e.g.*, household activities, health, education, housing, etc.).

- changes in the traditional attitudes towards women by enabling them to fully participate in scientific and technological development by stimulating their involvement in various forms of education and training.
- an increase of the level of scientific and technological self reliance by developing national scientific and technological potentials, maximisation of the possibilities for technical proporation among developing countries and the introduction of selective transfer of technology systems.
- establishment of linkages between the existing traditional technologies and know-how and the new technologies. The involvement of women in the strengthening of these links could provide a firm basis for self-reliance and ensure a certain continuity in the development of authentic and original approaches, thus avoiding imitative modernisation, and developing participatory research as well as relating scientific and technological development to the specific needs of the country.
- establishment and strengthening of cooperation among developing countries in the areas of information on scientific and technological knowledge and devices transfer of technology and exchange of experience on application of science and technology in development, joint research, etc.

Skills and Services

The term services or tertiary sector encompasses a wide range of activities. Therefore, the analysis of the role of women in the services sector covers the generally complex problem of services classification and data, the identification of the manpower problem in general, and women's hidden economic role in particular, and the relationship between the services sector and the overall economy of the country.

Over the last decades this sector's contribution to GDP increased substantially, not only in developed market economies but also in developing countries, where this upward trend was evident even in the least developed countries. The services sector accounted for the largest share of GDP in both developed market economies (56.9 percent) as well as in developing countries (44.3 percent). In developing countries the services sector expanded at a past faster rate than the GDP in the period 1973-80, implying that the general slowdown of their economies during these periods affected the services sector less severely than other major economic sectors.

However, the expansion of the services sector in developing countries, particularly in least developed countries, is probably due to quite different economic causes and could the attributed to the marginalisation of the labour force in agriculture and industry. The development of services is partly due to major changes in agriculture and industry, and partly to their heterogenous production and consumption characteristics.

The role of women in the tertiary sector is very difficult to determine. However, the distribution of the female labour force may serve as an indicator. The total female labour force in developing countries was employed in agriculture, in industry and in services. This is very different from the situation in developed countries, where the shares are for agriculture, for industry and for services. In developing countries the share of females in the total labour force, by economic sectors, was highest in agriculture and much lower in the services sector.

There are considerable disparities between developing countries in the different regions-disparities between Latin America on the one hand and Asia and Africa on the other. In Asia the main feature is the relatively high share of women in the total labour force in industry (28.8 percent) and the lower share in services (23.2 percent). In Latin America the low share of women in the total agricultural labour force (9.3 percent) is in sharp contrast to the situation in the other two regions. In this region female employment in the services sector is as high as 38.3 percent. In Africa women account for 31.6 percent of labour in services, while their share in industry is only 19.7 percent. (UNIDO, 1984).

Many of the service activities in which women are employed do not require formal technical qualifications. Other activities such as health (especially nursing) and education (especially teaching) do require professional qualifications, but these are in many cases considered an extension of the essentially female role which has its origin in the household-the mother care offered to the family. Thus women's contribution in this sector has not really been adequately recognised.

Much of the productive activity of women in the services sector remains invisible because of its mainly traditional and informal nature in developing countries. Some thought should be devoted to the services, which this sector could provide to meet the needs of households in this countries, that is, what the services sector should produce for the household and its members.

In view of the importance of the role of women in this sector and of the significance of the services sector for the improvement of the status of women in developing countries, it is suggested that:

- attention be paid to the analysis of the functioning, growth and development of the services sector (both public and private) in all developing countries, especially as regards the inter-linkages among this and all other sectors;

- the position of women in this sector should be viewed as developmental and integrative of other activities, which means that the new developmental trends observed in this sector must be closely linked to overall development and the advancement of women;
- services classification and data collection should be made more transparent and accessible;
- cooperation among developing countries in this sector, which is scattered over different areas and usually invisible being traditional and informal;
- women's hidden economic role in the services should be further studied and analysed;
- could be pursued with a view to the development of self-reliant schemes. Cooperation among developing countries in this sector could contribute to exchange of experiences, to development of self-reliant schemes and linkages between micro and macro levels of implementation. This may be an avenue for the promotion of new approaches to the development of the services sector.

Education and Training

Education is a double-edged instrument: it can contribute to and be an ally of structural changes in society by training people in required skills-old, newly emerging and anticipated. It is also a value-generating process influencing the behaviour, norms and cultural attitudes of people, particularly younger ones. From the beginning of the movement for the equality of women in recent history, great emphasis was placed on education as the major instrument for the elimination of gender inequality. Developing countries have viewed education as an instrument to stimulate development in all fields, and to reduce their dependence on external advisers. The basic problems were to promote a rapid expansion of development and cultural structures to meet the manpower requirements of development and cultural progress in general. Scarcity of resources and the shifting priorities of development have constrained the balanced pursuit of these aims.

Illiteracy still remains a major problem in most developing countries and women constitute a large proportion of the illiterates. About 60 percent of the approximately 800 million adult illiterates in developing countries are women. Although the proportion of illiterates in the total adult population has decreased, the results are still unsatisfactory. The absolute number of illiterates in these countries is still increasing. Gender differences persist among illiterates, especially because the lower enrolment ratios for girls at the elementary level increase the number of illiterate women. The gender gap among illiterates is increasing in developing countries.

Trends in the process of equalising the access of men and women to different levels of the educational system, as measured through enrolment ratios, show some interesting results. Over two decades the gender gap in enrolment ratios for the age groups 6-11 and 12-17 has remained virtually constant in developing countries, although there is overall improvement in entrolment for both sexes. At the higher level of education, the gap is much narrower, in contract to developed countries, where the gender gap exists mainly at the higher level. At this level the gender gap has shrunk in the developed countries during the last decade, and it has slightly widened in the group of developing countries.

The persistence of these gaps prevents the equalisation of educational opportunities with consequent effects on employment, skill acquisition and participatory opportunities in all fields. The widening of the gap in higher education is a matter of serious concern, because this sector is the training ground for entry into many areas important development, *e.g.*, science and technology, communication industries utilising high level technology, professions such as law, medicine, etc. It is also the training ground for most managerial and decision-making occupations.

The participation of women in decision-making positions, which is already limited, could shrink still further if this gap were to expand. In addition to resource constraints, educational progress in developing countries has been impeded by many other problems. Lack of harmony with productive and other developmental activities, which is often a consequence of borrowed models of educational systems, imposed the need to reform and adapt educational systems and institutions, to turn increasingly to the informal aspects of education (vocational training, on the job-training, etc.), and to introduce mass media and other modern devices as useful means of spreading equcational programmes and contents in an effort to reach as many social groups as possible.

Developing countries have been experiencing great problems in education, reflected in poor material basis and functional difficulties, in sometimes alarming dropout levels (especially in Sub-Saharan Africa and South Asia), in the fact that a substantial proportion of children are unable to read and write even after going to primary school for four or five years, etc. Women are still mostly employed in traditional and informal sectors where there has been a lower level of technological and information support. This further compounds their educational handicaps. However, women with education have entered many new areas of occupation where their participation was virtually non-existent before.

The enable women to participate actively in all spheres of economic and social life, vocational and professional training must be further developed. In this respect, the training of trainers is of primary importance, as is the introduction of management training for women. Apart from the conventional types of training (seminars, workshops, export group meetings training through doing, etc.), the non-conventional types are often also suitable. Of special relevance are also the new participatory types of training, which include learner-centered methods developed in the framework of non-formal education in which trainers are facilitators, to elicit productive response and interaction-and local social and cultural forms that can be built upon for effective training. These include decision making patterns, social groupings and communications networks.

Culture

The major lacunae in educational development are in the areas of cultural change and promotion of social values, which support and reflect the goals of development. Cultural transformations are taking place in developing countries, but in many cases through processes over which the people and even the governments have little control. New values and aspirations are often promoted, directly or indirectly, for profit maximisation—by forces inside or outside the country Changes in consumption patterns and role models are stimulated by mass media, commercial interests and a process of borrowing or emulation of life styles from developed countries. In many countries such changes have contributed to a widening of the gap between the elites and the masses of the people between the rural and urban populations, between the rich and the poor. This presents a challenge to the educational system, which must correct the trend if it is to promote the goals of participatory development, and collective self-reliance, eliminate the dependency on external support and contribute to comprehensive integrated development.

While there is evidence that the process of unplanned cultural change helps to promote illusory images, which are far removed from the social realities of developing countries, cultural reaction, which tries to counter these influences by looking only to the past, may also have a negative impact on development. In their efforts to preserve their cultural identities developing countries have sought to reaffirm their attachment to their cultural heritage. While pride in this heritage can contribute to the spirit and the value of self-reliance, this process may also lead to distortions—to a withdrawal from present-day problems and realities to a glamorisation of the past, to the imposition of the culture of dominant groups on other culturally diverse groups and to a strengthening of some of the forces and institutions that oppose the goals of comprehensive, participatory development of all peoples, classes and groups.

In view of the crucial importance of culture values in the dynamics of development, it will be essential to enhance the role of the women and to promote new cultural values that take into account existing social realities and support the efforts to build a different future. Integral development, which subsumes equal participation in development *i.e.,* in production and decision making will enhance the role of culture in the development context. Women will no longer be viewed as marginal producers (or providers of an auxiliary workforce), but rather as equal partners in the promotion of development.

Educational institutions will have to play an active role in the promotion of the development of such new cultural values. Hitherto, their contribution has been inadequate. Structurally pedagogically and philosophically, educational institutions will have to play a far more active role in the development of a new cultural context that can contribute to the realisation of the goals of comprehensive development—human and material. This also requires that they internalise the concern for the equality of women and the enhancement of their role—in their curricula, pedagogic methods, organisation and research agendas.

A strategic interrelationship between education and cultural and socio-economic development which integrates concern for the emancipation of women would have to be characterised by respect for the specific cultural features of a particular environment and clearly define the cultural and developmental function of education in social transformation and support the process of educational reform.

In this connection, the promotion of new knowledge about women and new perceptions of the role of women in development could be viewed as an instrument for educational and cultural development with a view to:

- strengthening and extension of training activities so as to embrace all relevant problems, such as: improvement of professional skills, education for family life and responsibilities, training for community organisation and management, decision waking etc.;
- promotion of integral and interdisciplinary links among developing countries in the field of cultural transformation and education and especially in professional and vocational training as well as in all forms of non-conventional training, to ensure availability of cadres capable of handling the new technology.
- equal participation of the local population, and particularly of women, in devising, deciding upon and implementing development programmes; this can be achieved by clearly defining the developmental interests of all groups of the population;
- enhancement of the collective self-reliance of nonaligned and other developing countries in culture

and education by intensifying their communication in these fields, especially as regards the methodologies for educational reform which incorporates the advancement of women as one of its concerns.

Mass Media

This section focuses on the possibilities which the media offer provided they are used judiciously to reflect the contribution which women are making to the nation's development efforts. Communication media have been a powerful social influence, both as instruments of change and for maintaining *status quo*. In the last decade, an impressive amount of literature on the portrayal of women in the media has been produced. These studies have expressed concern about the stereotyped and negative images of women, which are being projected through the media without any cognizance of the new and expanded roles of women in society. Communication media are a powerful tool for the creation of an alternative and positive image of women and could promote new attitudes and strategies for action directed towards the achievement of the goal of equality for women. It is imperative to democratises the control over the communication media and to make them an instrument for the creation of an awareness of women's needs and problems.

Mass media, especially the audiovisual media, play an important role by influencing the consumption patterns and life-styles, and usually promote commercial interests (often of external producers), thus creating pressures to distort trade and industrial policies. They also contribute to the distortion of cultural development, promoting imported values, which militate against comprehensive integrated development and the principle of collective self-reliance. There has been a recent trend among media professionals in developing countries towards greater realism in their portrayal of social problems. Realism, however, must be used to inspire people to struggle for change. A search for new options in human relationships, the reshaping of social institutions, political and economic structures and cultural values, would go a long way towards integrating women into the world of the media, and enable the media to play a more positive role in integrated development.

In the past, there has been a one-way flow of information from the developed to the developing countries, and from government to the people. The goals of self-reliance and participatory development, which are being actively pursued by the non-aligned countries, involve a shift from excessive reliance of the developing countries on foreign resources towards a mobilisation of their indigenous resources, which would make these countries less vulnerable to external pressures and develop their own potential for growth. The new information and communication technology, the microchip revolution, has considerably magnified the power of the media. Satellite communication has exposed millions of people to new information.

Women are today an important factor in the strategy of self-reliance and the media could do much to create public awareness of the role of women and their potentials. There are a number of steps, which the media could take at various levels to strengthen the role of women as equal partners in development:

- a democratisation of the structures and control of the communication media could contribute to the representation and participation of women in the media at the decision-making levels;
- more women should be involved in media training programmes; communication and advertising policies involving participation by women could be developed;

— listeners and viewers from consumer groups or NGO action groups, etc., could be effectively utilised to create an awareness of women's issues and to evolve common strategies for the promotion of more positive approaches to women's issues;

— media content could be improved through coordinated efforts for increased interaction between nongovernmental organisations in formulating guidelines for monitoring programmes;

— various international seminars, conferences and expert group meetings, which have already covered a wide range of issues connected with women and the communication media indicate the need for further in depth studies, research training for women in communication technology, the organisational framework, including the development of a code of ethics with regard to the presentation of women in media and using traditional folk media to encourage participation of women.

— horizontal communication and cooperation among developing countries in this field could be strengthened in order to create an awareness of issues of common concern, identifying solutions to common problems and areas of cooperation.

Development Issues

The still largely unresolved problems of the inter-connections between economic and social development and the increasing concern for the distributional and human dimensions of development indicate the need to pay more attention to all aspects of social development. The issues of health, social security, population trends and family planning, housing urbanisation and the environment, are linked with the general problem of the level of socio-economic development of a country its resource base and social policies.

Health Delivery Systems

Millions of people in developing countries are trapped in poverty, malnutrition, hunger and disease, although there are regional variations in living conditions. It is estimated that acute forms of potential energy malnutrition affect 35 percent school children in Africa, 16 percent in Asia and 4 percent in of Latin America. Similarly, it is estimated that two-thirds pregnant women in the developing world suffer from nutritional anaemia. High maternal and infant mortality rates are closely linked with inadequate maternal and child health care services, lack of proper sanitation and a safe drinking water supply. By the end of the last decade, only 42 percent of households in developing countries had access to a potable water supply and over three quarters of the population lacked access to sanitary facilities.

A disaggregation of social indicators by regions reveals that not only is there a very great gap between the developed and developing countries but also that their is great diversity among the developing regions. The average life expectancy in Sub-Saharan Africa is 47.4 years while it is 63.9 years in some Asian countries. Similarly, infant mortality is highest in Sub-Saharan Africa, while it is more in South East Asia. In the South Asian region the mortality differentials by sex indicate higher infant mortality among females and empirical data also show sex-based health and nutrition related behaviour. In the health care subsystems, there are interesting variations: Latin America—with the highest per capita GDP— has 7.5 physicians and 11. 7 nurses per 10,000 population, followed by some countries in South East Asia, where despite low GDP per capita the averages are 5.4 physicians and 5.2 nurses per 10,000 population.

Most developing countries are faced with the problem of a decline or slowing down of the growth rate of production, rising unemployment, growing deficits in balance of payments and inflation. All these adversely affect the availability of resources for social services, *i.e.*, health, education and social security.

Despite the methodological weaknesses of the existing social indicators and an absence of data on access to and distributional characteristics of the social development infrastructure, the trends indicate that results differ sharply also within regions and that social improvements definitely do not come automatically as a by product of economic growth. In many cases health resources are disproportionately concentrated in big cities, at the expense of primary health care for the masses in rural areas Problems requiring careful study include disparities in increase and living standards, and the care available to different social groups, inadequate planning and management of health development, problems of inter and intra-sectoral coordination, administrative decentralisation and involvement of the people in the planning, programming and implementation of health care programmes.

Very few developing countries have systems of social security. Even where such systems exist, a large part of the population in the informal sector—a substantial proportion of which are women-is not covered by the existing systems of mater benefits, health insurance, old age benefits, etc. In some countries voluntary and philanthropic organisations supplement state action. However, their work is often uncoordinated and not adequate to deal with the increasing, demands of urbanisation and poverty. The development of social protection is linked to changes in the development strategies and orientation directed towards the satisfaction of basic minimum needs the reduction and elimination of poverty, promotion of employment opportunities and improvement other working conditions of labour.

The global strategy of Health adopted by the Thirty Fourth World Health Assembly in 1981, which emphasises basic health protection, the primary health care approach and organisation of an effective health care and health information system, identified priorities for health cooperation and drew up an Action Programme, stressing the need for a review of a number of policy orientations in the areas of primary health care, health information and monitoring system, community involvement in health programmes, prevention of infectious diseases, development of national services of health care and health education, production, distribution and consumption of drugs and protection of the human environment.

On the basis of the Medium-Term Programme for Technical Cooperation among Developing Countries for Health for All and in view of the calls for an acceleration of the development of national health care capabilities and the establishment of local points for TCDC in the area of health some priority activities may be identified:

- introduction of effective health surveillance systems at the national level, of health indicators for target setting and formulation of national priorities and plans of action, and of appropriate Systems for assessing strengths and weaknesses of national health programmes;
- linking of health policies and programmes with economic development and those facilities which can directly reduce women's drudgery and work burden and directly improve their health situation, *i.e.*, provision of adequate housing, water supply, sanitation, health regulations at the work-place, and health protection of women, particularly those working in the informal sector of the economy who are not covered by social protection policies;
- integration of maternal and child health care with family planning services and accelerated development of national capacities through development of health

institutions and infrastructures and increase of the number of health experts and particularly health workers;

- promotion of health education and indigenous system of health care;
- involvement of women's organisations in primary health care activities and their representation on national and local health councils;
- promotion of health education and indigenous systems of health care;
- involvement of woman's organisations in primary health care activities and their representation on national and local health councils;
- introduction of TCDC programmes for the promotion of industries which are important for the development of health care systems. The developing countries could evolve suitable mechanisms for cooperation in training and development of human resources, collaborative research, joint programming, exchange of information and references, and exploring the application of low-cost technologies for water supply and waste disposal.

Demographic Factors

It is becoming increasingly obvious that population policies should be Implemented parallel with better health care and general socio-economic development as population Issues touch on very fundamental human values.

As the Mexico Conference on Population in 1984 stressed population strategies cannot be limited to the analysis of population trends, since there is a dynamic interrelationship between these and socio-economic transformations. Hence what is required is a set of coordinated strategies and activities for the promotion of economic development of the quality of life, human rights and in particular the fundamental right to individual choice.

The status of women and the advancement of their role in development remains a critical element in the achievement of these objectives. The persisting inequalities between men and women—which are evident in the higher incidence of poverty, unemployment and illiteracy among women—the limited range of employment categories offered to women, and the uneven sharing of borne and family responsibilities make it difficult for women to participate actively in the socio-economic development of the country.

There is sufficient evidence to show that it is lower income groups with a low level of literacy, low and insecure income and low health and nutritional levels which have larger families. This is points to a need for planning policies, which have a more integrated approach. Rapid population growth will affect the efforts of countries to achieve food security and to reduce pressure on the natural resources; also, its effects on urbanisation and on land and capital will exacerbate inequalities.

Many governments have launched subsidised family planning programmes. However, incentives are offered to encourage people to reduce family size. Experience has shown that a clinical approach, which threatens social values, beliefs and customs does not succeed and is actually a disincentive. To breakthrough the vicious circle of poverty, high fertility and mortality calls for a more careful and humane public policy with a judicious balance between individual choice and dignity and promotion of a sense of responsibility among parents to ensure a better future for all children. This could be further stimulated and promoted through various forms of technical assistance at various levels as well as enriched through mutual exchange of information and experience among developing countries.

Coping with Over Population: Women in the Cities

The rapid growth of cities in developing countries has created serious problems, since a large proportion of urban migrant workers are living in temporary hutments and settlements without adequate basic amenities. The growth of cities and the steep rise in rural-urban migration is a manifestation of imbalances in the location and expansion of productive activity. Women are particularly affected, as many of their activities are connected with their homes and bad housing and hygiene conditions are detrimental to both their own and their families health. The growth of cities has also created ecological problems. The growing demands of expanding cities have put undue pressure on natural resources, destroying the harmony between human beings and nature, and has led to a degradation of productive resources like water, land and forests.

The expansion of agriculture by clearing large tracts of forest has caused desertification due to severe soil erosion, a problem, which is extremely serious in Sub-Saharan Africa (Sahel), north-western Asia and the Middle East. Forests are crucial to the ecological life of many developing countries and deforestation has created serious problems, as the consumption of forest resources has exceeded replacement possibilities through natural growth. This has affected millions of rural households and the role of women in these households, as well as the nutritional level of the families. The human costs of malnutrition, famine and disruption in the lives of people seeking employment are a matter of serious concern.

Environmental issues conceiving the environment in its broadest social context are most relevant for women. The increasing marginalisation of certain sections of the population, growing poverty and deprivation of the masses, decreasing food production, the energy crisis and human environmental degradation in many developing countries are all symptoms of a pattern of growth and resource utilisation which is geared to existing power structures and prevents a large section of the population from satisfying its basic needs. The multidimensional problems facing developing countries are interconnected, but often these connection are not understood by those who formulate sectoral policies. In the long run, social development policies will have to be closely integrated with economic development policies and a strong commitment to the improvement of the quality of life. The methods and instruments of analysis and planning of socio-economic development should therefore take adequate account of environmental constraint.

INSTITUTIONAL ISSUES

Both the conceptual and sectoral parts of this study have indicated the basic features and tendencies of the changing role and status of women in developing countries. This was primarily the result of an analysis of the overall impact of development on the position of women in the societies of the developing countries and of the role of women in the developmental process. The effects of socio-economic development in individual sectors of the economy and public life have been identified and analysed. The endeavours at operationalisation of national development policies, including the integration of women in development raised the issue of instruments and institutions to implement these policies.

Issues addressed in this sections are: the role of government of public and private enterprises and of political participation and the role of women in decision-making processes as factors of development.

Government and Institution Effort

In principle, most governments have accepted the improvement of the social, political, economic and legal status of women, and the integration of women into development as desirable goals and planning objectives. The response of government, parliament and other political institutions at various levels to the need for the integration of women's issues into development plans is important for the effective implementation of appropriate strategies.

Country experiences indicate that during the UN Decade for Women many countries established governmental machinery, either as part of the existing administrative structures, as independent agencies (commissions, bureau, ministries) for women's affairs, or in the form of National Councils, which were extra-governmental organisations. Most of these mechanisms were created with the objectives of establishing responsibility and accountability within the government for planning, programming and implementing programmes for women and to act as a catalyst; providing the necessary infrastructure and resource support and training personnel: and reviewing, monitoring and evaluating policies and programmes and their impact on women.

The Mid-Decade review of the efficacy of these administrative and institutional mechanisms indicated that the constraints to action have ranged from conceptual of resource and organisational fractional factors. They do not have strong executive and resource support and have a limited mandate. The tendency has been to locate such units mainly within departments of social welfare and culture, which are considered non-productive and are usually not in the mainstream of the development effort and also suffer most from budgetary constraints during economic recession. The experience of some developing countries also indicates that the existence of governmental or state mechanism of this kind tends to reduce the concern of other administrative organs and of society as a whole for the advancement of women and leads to a diminution of activity in this direction.

As already indicated, the problems with regard to the role of women are closely linked with the problems of overall development. However, most of the governments have perceived the role of women as a specific interest issue without making any, attempt to integrate the problems involved into the mainstream of development planning. In many developing countries women-specific projects were designed to provide income-generating activities and basic needs to poor rural and urban women. These efforts basically addressed the immediate needs for survival faced by women in the poorer sections, without addressing the multidimensional and multisectoral processes and structures that marginalise these women. The governmental bodies deliberating on the crucial strategies of food production, industrialisation rural development, science and technology, and monetary reforms still face the problems connected with the integration of the role of women into their overall plans of action.

It is becoming increasingly evident that issues related to the position of women cannot meaningfully be dealt with only through specific projects, without effectively linking them to economic policies, plans and programmes, and making these projects an integral part of the long-term process of development. The typical women and development projects may, however, perpetuate the reformist stance by promoting marginal, often non-viable activities not linked to major sectors of development and sometimes lead to a considerable increase in women's burden without providing the necessary supportive institutions for their new role and expanded opportunities. They fail to deal with structural inequalities, which lead to changes in policies and programmes and affect the allocative, distributive and participatory processes.

The access of women to productive resources is a necessary precondition for their advancement. Recent discussions in both international and national flora have stressed issues such as title to land, access to credit and banking facilities, to employment on equal terms and under equal conditions, and to information and knowledge, education and training. Any policy aimed at improving the lot of poorer households should involve substantial changes in resource control, *e.g.*, land tenure, investment patterns, access to information regarding markets, technology, employment opportunities, availability of financial or other support, training etc., to increase women's control over their own labour and income.

During the UN Decade for Women, besides the integrative approach, arguments for specific transitional strategies and policies by the government to deal with the historically disadvantaged position of women were put forward. The approach was based on the assumption that the understanding of the role of women could be strengthened within the complex framework of government by setting time-specific and measurable goals within each important sector, thus operationalising the concern for the position and role of women and translating it into programmes of action. Further, recognising the close link between class and gender issues, it was expected that targetting for each group, in addition to the overall development target, would narrow the gender gaps in various sectors. To ensure a more meaningful intervention, a blending of the two approaches, *i.e.*, integral development with specific action, is suggested. Minor transitional activities should be in line with the long-term perspectives, if they are not to be counter-productive. A survey conducted by the ILO in mid-1984, on the integration of the question of women in national development plans, reveals that only 12 of 44 developing countries has incorporated employment of women by sectors in their national development plans, 28 countries had setup governmental bodies dealing with the question of female workers, and only 19 of 44 countries had undertaken sectoral surveys to investigate the problems and prospects of female workers. Much ground remains to be covered before the legal guarantees and administrative measures can be put into practice. Attempts at removing legal obstacles and improving access to education and other social services have not prevented growing poverty and malnutrition, rising unemployment and underemployment coupled with an increasing work burden, and persistent marginalisation of women in the economy and in decision making structures, although there have been varying results in the individual countries and regions.

However, governments have experienced considerable difficulties in their attempts to articulate these new approaches in policies and development action. These are due to a number of factors: the persistent invisibility of women as a critical and important factor within development structures; continued lack of awareness and understanding of the difficulties that women face even when they are participating on equal terms in development—both as beneficiaries and as agents; and delays in developing an adequate set of monitoring and evaluation measures and instruments to speed up effective implementation of adopted policies.

The most urgent task, which now faces governments is more innovative blending of the role of women into the design of action programmes, policy instruments and evaluation criteria or monitoring procedures in all sectors of development. The issue of women's role in development cannot be a concern of women only. The value-creating mechanisms, *i.e.*, the educational system, and the media, may be suitably modified to project values of sex equality. Governments could modify or eliminate legal provisions that still uphold the unequal status of women.

The strategies for action suggested in the sectoral chapters all call for operational instruments. Who is to initiate, implement and evaluate these measures at the national and at the regional and international levels? The emphasis should be on perceptional, organisational and infrastructural development. At the government level, executive and administrative measures need to be taken to ensure recognition of women's productive, reproductive and participatory roles and to provide supportive services such as child care and need social services, *i.e.*, health care, education, catering, housing and drinking water, etc., to reduce their work burden and enable them to assume wider responsibilities.

What kind of policy instruments have been effective in incorporating the role of women into sectoral structures? A concerted effort is needed to bridge the gap between the highest levels of government and the intermediate and lower levels where plans are operationalised. A comparicon of organisational and infra-structural models and approaches in different countries could provide an insight into the strengths and weaknesses of various arrangement.

The Mexico Conference had visualised the National Commission as watchdog bodies—to review and recommend measures necessary to enhance the equality and participation of women in development and decision making. Some countries have defined the functions of the national mechanisms in this manner and provided them with the requisite powers of resource support. At the same time the strength of the argument that women's affairs cannot be separated from the sectoral agencies responsible for planning and implementation of development in the fields of agriculture and rural development, industry, energy, science and technology, urban and rural development, education, health and other social services must be acknowledged. Since the objective is the integration of women in all these sectors of development, it could be useful to institutionalise this concern, or mandate—to continue the task of making the Sectoral agencies sensitive, concerned and accountable.

In view of the stagnation of overall development, the modest resource support has kept efforts to promote the role of women at a marginal level in most developing countries. Thus in some developing countries such efforts have been primarily dependent on international aid. Apart from the fact that this may have precluded the integration of these efforts into major development sectors, this dependence has in some cases also diverted attention from the goals of collective and national self-reliance, and sometimes also distorted national priorities.

Research on women in development, which has evolved during the Decade as an important instrument for the advancement of the role of women has been useful, since it has been instrumental in the collection of empirical information which has, to date, provided most of the data to assess the impact of various development policies on women; it has sensitised the people involved in development planning and administration by posing issue resulting from their empirical investigations and promoted an ideological climate and public concern thus raising the level of consciousness among women and others.

So far, such studies have primarily been confined to research and have made little impact on the training and value transformation of younger generations. The promotion of such studies as an instrument for enhancing the role of women in development, through educational and training institutions agencies responsible for research and information has emerged as a critical need. Such an approach would be most appropriate within the areas of cooperation among the non-aligned countries in order to eliminate the dependence on external aid-with the possible risk of distortions. In view of the fact that the role of women in development has been acknowledged as an important component of the research and information system that is being promoted within the movement of the non-aligned countries, it is suggested that this component could be included through a combination· of research, training and information dissemination.

The incorporation of the aspects of the role of women in development in existing teaching/training and research institutions may reduce investments in physical and administrative infrastructure—and improve the prospects for integrating/articulating women's problems, issues and concerns within all educational institution/disciplines, instead of allowing them to remain a separate, marginal activity, whose isolation makes it ineffective. National, regional and international networks of such institutions should be encouraged to share and expand share and expand their experiences, which would help to increase their competence, and strengthen the ties or intellectual and developmental co-operation among non-aligned nations. Such efforts would help to increase the extent and improve the quality of data needed by national governments. They would also make it possible to train an increasing number of cadres to take up the various functions identified as necessary for the advancement of women in development. Above all, the incorporation of studies of this kind within the educational systems and in training institutions would help promote the needed cultural transformation. Science and technology, which could be powerful instruments for the advancement of the role of women in development have so for usually by passed women because their educational and other handicaps. Science and technology have also often been misused to marginalise women and reduce their status. It is therefore important not merely to facilitate the access of women to science and technology, but also to ensure that practitioners will be aware of the problems involved in the employment of women in his areas. It would be useful to introduce these concerns as early as the training stage.

In particular, developments in the fields of communication technology and communication sciences pose a critical challenge to the decisions of the non-aligned Countries to enhance the role of women in development. If these new developments are not harnessed in accordance with the policies for the advancement of women, they will continue to be used by social forces, which oppose the equality of women and development, and help to strengthen and perpetuate values and behavioural norms that thrive on the subordination of women.

The improvement of the systems for data collection and development of quantitative and indicators for measuring women's development is another critical area. Despite repeated decisions at various international conferences many national data collection agencies still do not have adequate data on women, nor do they provide sex break-downs or gender differentiation in different fields. They continue to be pervaded with a biased understanding of what is important information regarding the status of women and its impact on the conditions and equality of life of families, communities and development in general. Similarly, there has been little follow-up action at the national levels to the very useful international efforts and decision to develop and compile comparable socioeconomic indicators to measure the role of women in development, as initiated recently by INSTRAW and the UN Statistical Office.

A system of reporting by sex disaggregated data would help the flow of information from the bottom up, monitoring the actual implementation of programmes and benefits accuring to women, and through women to the entire community, and increase the accountability of government agencies. Simultaneously, such a process would initiate improvement of data systems, concepts and methods of statistics and development of indicators.

Numerous studies from developing countries have demonstrated the importance of women's grass-root participatory organisations. When genuinely participatory they become dynamic instruments—not merely for the advancement of women, but for the improvement of the quality of the development process as a whole. But in many developing countries; such organisations have not yet been evolved. Where women's cooperatives, village level organisations and voluntary agencies to exist, they generally receive little support in the way of resources, information or recognition.

In acme cases, the efforts of non-governmental organisation have provided some support to break the isolation of these grassroot groups. The NGOs have often played the role of an intermediary, providing the needed support to the grassroot groups helping to establish direct communications between them and development agencies, and also helping to develop networks of grassroot groups to enable them to learn from each other. An important strategy for governments to consider is recognition of some organisation/institutions as intermediaries to increase the governments' reach, to obtain the needed feed-back from the grass roots and to raise the level of information and knowledge at both ends.

The concept of intermediaries provides a new channel for organisation/institutions outside the government to playa role in advancing the status of women in development and help operationalise some of the strategies already accepted. The concept of an autonomous intermediary—supported by government resources and acting as a channel of communication between grass-root groups and government without the negative features of a patron-client relationship at either end-officers an operational instrument to implement some of the accepted strategies.

Strategies to further strengthen the role of women in the overall development efforts could be oriented towards:

- continuation and redoubling of efforts to make the role of women visible in various sectors of development, in various agencies and instruments for government action, such as the leglslatures the judiciary, planning agencies, public enterprises, specialised agencies created by governments for particular aspects of economic and social development, financial institutions, etc.;

— reviewing, monitoring and evaluating policies and programmes and their impact on women in development and *vice versa*—from an integrated and coordinated point of view;

— provision of the necessary infrastructure, resource and cadre support for planning and execution of the governmental policies in this regard;

— promotion of value transformation, in view of the long-term objective of the advancement of the role of women in development;

— enhancement of the opportunities for women to take part in decision making as fully informed citizens;

— further research and training of all those involved and concerned in promoting the status of women information gathering systems should be promoted in order to provide essential inputs for government policies and actions;

— access of women as well as of men, to information on the decisions taken by their governments, on available assistance and support and agencies and structures from which to obtain such support;

— exchange of information and experience, as well as consultative arrangements at venous levels, particularly at the regional and inter-government levels. In this matter a number of international, regional or interregional institutions might be requested to assist the identification of communication channels;

- raising of the literacy level and upgrading and dissemination of knowledge. This is where communication technology and traditional communication channels should be harnessed;

- elaboration of guidelines for all bilateral and multilateral technical cooperation programmes to ensure the incorporation of elevant aspects of the role of women in development. The UNDP Indicative Planning Figure should also incorporate these aspects for basic programmatic action;

- inclusion of the question of the role of women in development in the preparation of plans for negotiations at all stages of the project cycle at different levels of regional and international cooperation, so as to ensure that the result of these projects will not be in conflict with national objectives;

- incorporation of a social impact analysis into all projects to avoid negative results, Non-aligned countries cooperation could help to develop the necessary methodology for such analyses;

- continuaticn of the work already initiated by national and international research institutions in refining and building up an adequate analysis (conceptual and methodological) and identification of indicators which can measure the work done by women, especially in food production and agriculture. Data (time series data should reflect the real position of women within the context of overall long-term trends in development. Research should include gender-specific analysis to illustrate the types of inequality which still require measures to overcome them.

●●●

6

Basic Concept of Empowerment

The empowering of women is necessary sustainable development of a community. Sustainability implies a state of balance and equilibrium in factors related to human life which can be social, political, financial, environmental and even spiritual. It is a state to which all those factors that influence the process of the growth of human being and her/his holistic environment has to advance in unison but independently, yet supporting each other. In the case of a woman equality, social justice and freedom have dynamic roles to achieve such sustainability. But the notion of sustainability often become the victim of unsustainable traditions and political opportunism. If a human being is forced to live in an inhuman and degrading condition, sustainable development becomes unattainable. Hence, corruption, nepotism, violence, inequality, exploitation and oppression are counter-productive to sustainable development.

Projects was undertaken in slums in Nagpur City in India. The social workers were constantly in touch with the people of these slums. These social workers with the active participation of the slum people, especially of women and youth, arranged a number of public meetings, discussions and dialogues. These get-togethers helped us to understand the people, their life-patterns, values, cultural inhibitions, weakness, strength, etc. The regular group meetings and discussions enabled the people to be more realistic and helped them to understand common problems in collective way rather than viewing them individualistically.

The intimate and probing sharing of ideas with youth and women by our social workers helped us to understand them. Many of the youths believed that certain changes were required for their socio-economic and human development, but they were not quite sure about the quality and quantity of these changes. They were ready for action, but were in need of emotional, intellectual and to a certain extent financial support to achieve their goals. Most of the youths, and a great majority of women were eager to have a better life. The slum dwellers, even though capable of change and growth, were anxious of social change, which might bring about uncertainties. They had be helped to free themselves from traditions which were detrimental to their progress, superstitions and other types of oppressions. Concerted action was necessary to help these people to get out of their lethargy, fatalistic beliefs, in human poverty and internal as well as external oppressions. To help these slum dwellers, especially the women and youth for richer and fuller life and bring about meaningful sustainable human development external help was imperative.

The Project envisaged the people of these slums to understand the meaning of their lives and their inner potentialities. The, women of these communities were in need of professional help to get out of their sluggishness, fear, lethargy and superstition. In the same way, the youth too were in need of help to perceive their real ability and capacity. The Agency believed that the projects would create a meaningful and action-oriented awareness among the women and youth. It would also help them to think and act about their values, institutions and other structures, which dominate the life of the people. The Projects would be ushered by women and youth of these slums. They themselves would work to achieve the aims, according to their felt needs and priorities. It implies the active involvement of each and every child, youth, woman and man of these slums.

Awareness creation would lead towards social and economic development of women. It also include the development of local leadership. It helps to develop self-reliant and self-sustaining men and women of these communities. The action oriented awareness which the women of these communities achieve would be dynamic and progressive. Critical thinking resulting in sustainable development is the goal of this awareness. The Projects would help women to understand themselves, to know their surroundings and the various situations in which they were. It would give an opportunity to evaluate their lives in comparison with others. The Projects had inbuilt potential to bring about substantial changes in the quality of lives of women in these slums. The Projects had proposed a dynamic and growth oriented participation of the community especially that of women. It would be the Projects of women and youth. Their active participation was envisaged in every step of the planning and implementation. The objectives would be achieved by the efforts of women alongwith the full involvement Community Action for Development. The Project had proposed through its objectives, the creative and growth oriented participation of women and youth of these slums. To work towards the socio-economic development of women and their empowerment for a sustainable development of themselves as well as the communities in which they lived and worked was the main objective of the Project. The specific one were:

(a) To create awareness among women and youth on their present condition and to bring out their opinion on the causes of their problem and help them to suggest possible remedies.

(*b*) To Organise women for the betterment of their family and community.

(*c*) To encourage women and youth to think and act and help to develop in them hope and spirit of hardwork and self-help.

(*d*) To help the most vulnerable groups in the communities' especially girls through specialised vocational training programmes so that they could be catalysts to change.

(*e*) To help authorities to organise basic health and educational services for children and women.

(*f*) To organise special training for children to develop human resources through pre-school and school dropouts education and other programmes.

(*g*) To provide specialised services to the needy such as alcoholics, anti-social elements and to those individuals and groups who have socio-psychological problems which prevent them to integrate themselves in the general community.

(*h*) To start with the active participation of the community, social and informal education and vocational training programmes mainly for youth and women.

(*i*) To organise the women so as to form Mahila Mandals and to help them to have self-employment income generation programmes.

(*j*) To enable income generation and self-employment programmes among women so that the community can achieve sustainable development.

(*k*) To encourage the community self-help and lead themselves for sustainable development.

(l) To develop local leadership and democratic values and empower women to take decisions affecting them.

Main Problems

The following are the main problems identified by CAD with the help of the people of these slums:

(a) Women and youth had insufficient awareness on their capacity to change, develop and the potentialities of local leadership.

(b) Apathetic attitude and lack of motivation to social, psychological and economic change or understand the need and nature of such change.

(c) Ignorance of basic human needs, priorities and human development.

(d) Deep ignorance of social, cultural, economic and political conditions, which enslave them.

(e) Unorganised nature of the slum population and exploitation by outsiders.

(f) Unemployment or lack of any steady income for at least one member in the family.

(g) Lack of skills to do work.

(h) Overcrowding of the single room huts as well as the slum.

(i) Illiteracy, drug addiction, alcoholism, family breakdown, delinquency, crime, etc.

(j) Void of purposiveness in life, especially among young people.

(k) Absence of civic facilities such as water supply, electricity, sewerage facility, etc.

(*l*) Isolation from the mainstream of life and resultant lack of facilities for self-employment and income generation programmes.

(*m*) Lack of facilities for pre-school, primary school education; non-formal, social and informal education.

(*n*) Ignorance to basics of healthcare, hygiene and nutrition and dominance in superstitious beliefs.

(*o*) Lack of concern towards children and their emotional, physical, intellectual and educational development.

(*p*) Health problems and lack of health care facilities for women.

(*q*) As the slums are unauthorised, the people are always feel threatened of eviction from the slums by the authorities.

(*r*) Caste and religious conflicts and political rivalries and resultant absence of community spirit and feeling of oneness.

(*s*) Ignorance and lack of faith in democratic values and decision-making.

(*t*) Unproductive or destructive tendencies among youth.

(*u*) Enslavement of women.

The Agency envisaged various programmes to achieve objectives of the Projects. The main ones are given below:

(*i*) Negotiate with the authorities to authorise the slums, so that the Nagpur Municipal Corporation may be able to provide the basic facilities such as water supply, sewerage facilities, electricity, etc.

(ii) Provision of help to have health services for the infants and children through organising immunisation, child health programmes, pre-natal and post-natal care, clinical services, etc. and establish health educational facilities for women and children.

(iii) Create awareness of the problems of the slum through discussions, dialogues, community meeting, observations, etc.

(iv) Conducting balwadis with community participation and enabling the eligible children to get enrolled in the schools. Pressurising the Municipal Corporation of Nagpur City to start new primary school facilities in or adjacent to the slums.

(v) Establish rapport with youth of the community and help them to start self-employment and income generation programmes.

(vi) Organise civic services through women and youth in collaboration with the Municipal Corporation of Nagpur City.

(vii) After studying the possibilities of self-employment and income generation programmes, take initiatives in getting the most needy people trained and then help in establishing in self-employment programmes.

(viii) Organise women and create awareness on the need of better, health, adult education, education of children, income generations programmes, etc.

(ix) Regular meetings and action oriented discussions about alcoholism, gambling, wife-battering, child marriage, dowry, drug addiction, etc.

(x) Organise slums committees, specifically with the help of youth and women, so that people can

understand and solves the various problems facing the community.

(xi) Arrange various types of awareness creation and training programmes for women.

(xii) Initiate informal action groups in each community for youth and women and organise regular discussions, meetings so as to enable them to bring forth their problems, need and type of solution that could be offered with the help. These action groups will also act as watch dogs against exploitation and oppression.

(xiii) Group dynamic programmes and introduction of games, role plays, etc., which may apparently encourage motivation in youth and women.

(xiv) Usage of mass media like exhibitions, slide shows, discussions, dialogues, so that women and youth will be enlightened.

(xv) Arranging counselling, casework and group work facilities.

(xvi) Organising regular informal and social education classes for selected women groups on self-help, sustainable development, quality of life, etc.

(xvii) Conscious effort to invoke voluntarism from the community.

(xvii) Providing regular case work help and counselling for alcoholics, drug addicts and those who are having family problems.

(xix) Organising referral services in all the aspects of socio-economic and sustainable development and establish permanent link with other organisations and agencies.

(xx) Help the women to assume responsibilities.

Phase-wise Programme Implementation

Each Project is envisaged for three years. The Agency believes that the objectives of the programmes can he achieved within the time span. The action plan is given below:

First Six Months

(a) Survey and study of the slum communities and by comparing the developmental level with other developed areas.

(b) Individual and family contact, contacting local leaders and identifying leaders.

(c) Analysing and understanding the most vital needs of the communities.

(d) Contacting women and understanding family needs and problems.

(e) Contacting men to understand their fears and problems.

(f) Contacting youth and understanding their aspirations and problems.

(g) Formation of women groups and youth clubs.

(h) Formation of Slum Communities with members of men, women and youth.

(i) Formation of workers' groups such as daily labours, coolies, construction workers, etc., for discussion of their specific problems.

(j) Inviting Government officials to the slums and having dialogue with them regarding the civic facilities and amenities and organising meetings of people with officials.

(k) Initiating Balwadis, Action Groups, etc.

Next Twelve Months

(*a*) Conducting regular social education sessions to make the people aware of their civil, social responsibilities and duties.

(*b*) Providing various services to the needy through existing Mahila Mandals and Youth Action Groups.

(*c*) Identify leaders from the community and organising developmental programmes.

(*d*) Identifying the most needy people, especially women and youth for self-employment and development of skills.

(*e*) Initiating adult and functional education classes.

(*f*) Involving the community in various activities.

(*g*) Purposeful participation of the community, especially of women and youth in various programmes.

(*h*) Organising various intensive training programmes.

(*i*) Initiating new mahila mandals.

(*j*) Giving responsibility to community health workers, community volunteers and balwadi teachers in various activities.

(*k*) Organising training programmes for mothers, unmarried girls, etc.

Next Twelve Months

(*a*) Initiating vocational training for youths.

(*b*) Initiating co-operatives for women.

(*c*) Intensifying social education and informal education.

(*d*) Strengthening community voluntarism and initiative.

(e) Strengthening income generation programmes and self-employment programmes.

(f) Organising various training programmes for youth, women and children.

(g) Creating awareness among men, women and youth for action.

(h) Organising youth programmes which help community feeling and belongingness.

(i) Organising programmes such as role play, street play, discussion, dialogue, etc., to have reflection, action and development.

(j) Orientation and training programmes for women to start their own self-employment programmes.

(k) Encouraging women to conscientise their men-folk and children.

(l) Intensive training to local leaders to think and act according to their own reflections based on community's genuine needs.

(m) Intensive community dialogue on its problems for the reconstruction of a better and healthy community life.

(n) Help the youth for democratic decision-making and Self-government.

Last Six Months

(a) Expanding the scope of supplementary income generation and self-employment programmes.

(b) Strengthen self-employment programmes.

(c) Strengthening the Mahila Mandals, youth action groups to take up the responsibilities.

(*d*) Partial withdrawal of the Agency from the community.

(*e*) Giving more responsibility to local leaders, women groups ana youth groups.

(*f*) Preparing women and youth to take up responsibilities.

(*g*) Intensifying awareness and action programmes organised by local leaders and youth groups.

(*h*) Dialogue organised by women and youth on democratic participation, decision-making, etc.

(*i*) Community leaders action oriented dialogue with rest of the community.

(*j*) Registration of slum committees.

(*k*) Democratic participation of people in their own development.

(*l*) Withdrawal of the Agency from the community.

All programmes were need based and implemented by the beneficiary community. Women formed the core of such beneficiary group and they also played the role of animators and catalysts.

Content of Leadership Training

The following were the general contents: There was flexibility according to specific needs and requirements.

(*a*) The concept of grassroots/local leadership; need and its importance.

(*b*) Developing local leadership.

(*c*) People's potential and their rights.

(*d*) Developing local participation.

(*e*) Constitutional rights, dignity of women.

(*f*) Role of local women in problem-solving.

(*g*) Nature and characteristics of dignity of women; exploitation of women in various communities.

(*h*) Women as leaders.

(*i*) Youth leadership.

(*j*) Areas of under development; women's oppression.

(*k*) Local women's intervention in community conflict/ anti-social activities.

(*l*) Sustainable development and women.

(*m*) Organising the Community, seeking external help, developing basic skills in dealing with people.

(*n*) How to contact the agencies; writing representations; conducting meetings; oraganising processions; programmes; etc.

(*o*) Developing awareness of human needs.

(*p*) Contacting women and understanding their reactions.

(*q*) Developing skills in self-help.

(*r*) Conducting evaluations.

Methods

(*i*) Talks, discussions;

(*ii*) Workshops;

(*iii*) Role play, Street play;

(*iv*) Film/slide show;

Motivational Training Programmes Content

(a) The inherent dignity of women.

(b) Reasons for backwardness of women:

(i) Historical, *(ii)* Social, *(iii)* Psychological, *(iv)* Cultural, *(v)* Political, *(vi)* Personal, *(vii)* Other reasons.

(c) Personality development and factors of motivation:

(i) Self-reliance *(ii)* Self-esteem *(iii)* Emotional development *(iv)* Awareness of self *(v)* Awareness of others and their problems etc.

(d) Importance of Women's Leadership:

(i) Leaders as servants *(ii)* Leaders as catalysts *(iii)* Leaders as inspiring persons *(iv)* Leaders as uniting force.

(e) Attitude towards life:

(i) Fatalism and resignation of women *(ii)* Hope, desire to develop, etc.

(f) Awareness:

(i) Games people play *(ii)* Defence mechanisms.

(g) Human aspirations:

(i) Basic rights *(ii)* Constitutional and legal protection of human rights.

(h) The role of education for a higher level of aspiration.

(i) Contact with community members as well as others.

(j) Transmission of information.

(k) Impact of audio-visual aids.

(*l*) Family and family responsibilities.

(*m*) Sharing and group discussions.

(*n*) Any other topic relevant to the situation.

Methods

(*a*) Socio-psychological games;

(*b*) Personal contracts;

(*c*) Case work;

(*d*) Group activities;

(*e*) Group work;

(*f*) Discussions;

(*g*) Use of audio-visual aids;

(*h*) Legal aid and discussion based on actual incident;

(*i*) Roll plays; street plays;

(*j*) Contents analysis based on newspaper reports;

(*k*) Analysis of human situations;

(*l*) Evolving practical solutions for everyday problems.

Contents of Vocational Training and Self-employment

(*a*) Need for vocational training, adopting self-employment.

(*b*) Various types and avenues of self-employment.

(*c*) Motivation to self-employment, creation of reality consciousness.

(*d*) Resource mobilisation in self-employment, loans, refund of loans procedures, etc.

(*e*) Standard of living and income generation.

(*f*) Budgeting.

(*g*) Savings and investment.

(*h*) Expanding the business.

Methods

(*a*) Talks, discussions.

(*b*) Demonstrations.

(*c*) Workshops.

(*d*) Field visits to agencies.

(*e*) Evaluations.

Training for Unmarried Girls

(*a*) Youth as a learning period.

(*b*) Social responsibilities.

(*c*) Importance of being the member of a larger community.

(*d*) Preparations for the future, development of a person.

(*e*) Problems of adolescence, social psychological, effective handling of oneself.

(*f*) Education, economic independence.

(*g*) Setting goals for life.

(*h*) Learning various skills, opportunities for vocational training.

(*i*) Preparation for family life, interpersonal relationship, friendship, parental responsibilities.

(*j*) Impact of surroundings on personality development.

(*k*) Special problems of unmarried slum girls.

(*l*) Proper utilisation of income; priorities and goals.

(*m*) Proper guidance and motivation.

(*n*) Anti-social activities and consequences.

(*o*) Community help to unmarried girls.

(*p*) Any other matter relevant to their lives.

Social Education

(*a*) Identifying the problems of self, group, community causes of problems, analysis, evaluation.

(*b*) Community spirit and leadership.

(*c*) Community action.

(*d*) Awareness, guidance on problems, seeking external help, etc.

(*e*) Importance of organised action, unity.

(*f*) Perspectives on development.

(*g*) Exploitation, occupational problems, gainful employment.

(*h*) Income utilisation, budgeting.

(*i*) Basic needs, services, health education, etc.

(*j*) Communal/caste disharmony.

(*k*) Social problems, alcoholism, clime, etc.

(*l*) Any other that are relevant.

Time Schedule and Evaluation

The Agency believed that the objectives of the Projects could be achieved within three years. The budget was prepared on the basis of this assumption. All the programmes given in the Project proposals were intensive and were carried out according to the time schedule mentioned in the Project proposals. It was the endeavour of CAD to achieve the objectives in time and make the project scientific, purposeful and absolutely people oriented. Every six months evaluation had been done on the basis of the rationale, nature and objectives of the project. The evaluation was factual and included all aspects of the project. The community people and project staff were actively involved in the evaluation. Evaluation reports were submitted to the sponsors of different Projects.

The following staff members were appointed for the projects.

(a) Director:	Overall incharge of the Project, under whose guidance the programmes were implemented. She prepared the reports and evaluation and responsible for financial aspect of the Projects.
(b) Co-ordinator:	She was a post-graduate in social work and worked with people in full time in the community. She organised all the programmes with the help of the people.
(c) Community:	She was a professional social worker and assisted the Director and Co-ordinator, organising various programmes.
(d) Grassroots:	They were from the community itself and worked shoulder workers to shoulder with the other project staff in the preparation, implementation and evaluation of the programmes.

To seek economic independence for every woman had been foremost objective of each project. The Agency realised that a job centred socio-economic development, which had faith in social justice and equality, would provide self-respect to women and initiate and strengthen the empowering of women and the resultant sustainable development.

Empowering Rural Women Through Floriculture

Flowers were not of much economic importance. One would grow flowers to fulfill one's aesthetic sense. With the passage of time, there has been great change in life-style of people leading to commercialisation of flowers growing. Today floriculture is recognised as a lucrative business since it has higher potential per unit area than most of the field crops even horticultural crops both for domestic market and export. The floriculture industry has a bright future as the global floriculture trade is growing at a very fast pace in the recent years. The world floriculture market is growing at an annual growth potential of 25-30 percent foreign exchange earning ability than cereals.

With the implementation of World Trade Organisation (WTO) provisions, the floriculture has received an impetus in recent years and it is emerging as major enterprise in world trade. Globally, trade of floriculture products is estimated to be US$ 52.24 million of which flowers and plants accounts for more than 80 percent of total trade.

More than 140 countries are now involved in floriculture. The share of developed countries is about 91 percent where as developing countries contributes only 9 percent in world trade of ornamentals. Inspite of having diverse soil, suitable agroclimatic conditions, large and reputed tissue culture facilities, expert and cheap manpower and developed industrial base, yet Indian share in world floriculture trade is less than one percent. It is because, serious attention was not paid in the past to develop trade on scientific line to exploit its full potentialities. Efforts on promoting commercial floriculture have started due to liberalisation of industry and trade policies. Government of India has identified floriculture as an 'Extreme Focus Segment Item' during the Eighth Five-year Plan and has allocated an amount of Rs. 100 million for its development. It is taking various steps to remove some of the constraints and assist this sector to participate in floriculture export. Total export of floriculture during 2000-2001 was Rs. 105.49 crore. There is a vast scope for domestic market of around (estimated) Rs. 500 crore, in 2002. Delhi's market's share being about Rs. 50 crore annually. The total area under floriculture in India was 88,529 ha during 1999-2000 with production of 5,09,193 tonnes of loose flowers and 680.57 million of cut flowers. A beginning has been made recently. However, the flower production activities have been taken extensively only in few states till now. The major states being Karnataka, West Bengal, Tamil Nadu, Andhra Pradesh, Maharashtra, Uttar Pradesh, Rajasthan, Haryana and Punjab having the largest area under flower production. Floriculture is popular in Haryana and cultivation of flowers is being taken up in the state on commercial lines and is turning more lucrative than other conventional agricultural crops. Haryana state have 2250 ha area with production of 40,500 tonnes of loose flowers and 76.00 millions cut flowers. It is very surprising that in 1962, there was only 4,000 ha. land under flower cultivation which increased up to 88,527 ha. in 2000 (ICAR, 2002).

In recent years, a few large business houses have entered into floriculture for the production of cut flower for home consumption as also for export. However, the production and trade of floriculture for traditional and industrial purpose is mainly in hands of small family enterprises, where women folk is prominent worker, the poorer the family, the more it depends on economic productivity of its women. They have invisible hand, 90 percent of rural women are unskilled and 88 percent are illiterate which makes them vulnerable to exploit and economically dependent on men. No serious efforts have been made to improve the condition of women in our country. It is possible through empowerment of women. There is need to train women for the floriculture oriented enterpreneurship through which women of rural areas can easily earn money in short run by this occupation. Till now no training is given on floriculture even to men folk then what will be place of women. If women would be trained for the job related to flower cultivation, future prospect of floriculture would be brighter and so will be national development.

Keeping in view the increasing demand and better returns from flowers than agricultural crops, Haryana State Government has started taking steps to popularize commercial cultivation of flowers in 1993 to earn foreign currency. Sonepat is leading district in Haryana state which have large area under flower cultivation and in Panipat district, there is much potential for flower production. Both districts have proximity to national capital market of flowers.

●●●

7

Issues of Women Empowerment

Women are discriminated on all walks of life. They are mistreated, underestimated and underscored. Disadvantages against women are commonly practices in the opportunities of socio-economic development, participation in different activities, availing educational facilities and various other development programmes associated with improving the life style and the quality of life, because of several social and cultural backwardness. Besides this, women are also denied the rights in the decision-making process in their family affairs on account of social and cultural constraints imposed by their family and the continuation of traditional system of civilization. Restrictions are also imposed in the participation of women in certain social and cultural programmes and to move outside households for certain purposes. As a result of these underlined problems imposed by our traditional society against women their participation in different activities, education, employment, political systems etc. has been very poor even after fifty years of independence. The condition of women in rural areas is far behind and more dissatisfactory than in urban areas on account of greater backwardness and the prevelence of traditional social and cultural system of society. The traditional form of society is keeping open different types of opportunities for their male family members only while the women are marginalised. In fact, the women are seriously exploited by men for certain purposes although most household related activities are performed by women in the rural area as of the country.

Similar disadvantage in employment and other activities linked with betterment of life is commonly observed in the case of women on account of the socio-cultural constraints imposed by households and discrimination practised by the employers. At the same time, restriction imposed against women in utilising own rights independently and social compulsion to make movements only for certain distances impose limitations in the availing opportunity of gainful employment of women. In addition to this, the discrimination against women in employment is largely a result of social values, which tend to place women in a secondary position and under subjugation of men. Also inspite of having similar level of educational attainment and productive efficiency for performing any economic activity or needed for any occupation the employer practicise a discriminatory behaviour against women.

After Indpendence, provisions were made in the Indian Constitution to provide equal rights and opportunities of socio-economic development and betterment of living for men and women, including different disadvantaged segment of population to establish an egalitarian and prosperous society. In view of bringing improvements in the socio-economic condition of women efforts were made to maximise the participation of women in different educational levels, with the notion that education is the most important instrument to bring awareness about their rights, social status, as a prime element to maximise participation in different categories of remunerative employment etc. This goal of increasing participation in education was sought to be achieved by planning for introducing subsidised educational facilities, expansion of girls educational curriculum according to the need and requirements of girls, recruitment of women teachers and providing various other facilities. In addition to this, various development programmes were also introduced, specially for women, in the various plans during the past with the intention that the participation of women in different development programmes could be increased at certain extent.

The Directive Principle of State Policy enshrined in the constitution have a special bearing on the status and empowerment of women. The Constitution guarantees political equality to women through the institution of adult franchise. This recognisation was certainly a radical departure from socio-cultural norms of the traditional Indian society. In the past various legal reforms were, therefore, initiated to improve the status of women in the typical Indian social system and to strengthen the women's empowerment. Important reforms in this direction were Hindu Marriage Act, Hindu Succession Act, Hindu Adoption and Maintenance Act, Hindu Minority and Guardianship Act, Dowry Prohibition Act, Maternity Benefit Act etc.

During the Women Decades the women were promised that various development schemes and reforms would be introduced at the policy level to provide more respectable status to women in Indian society. Most important laws and status of women were Equal Remuneration Act, Marriage Law Amendment Act, The Child Marriage Restrain' (Amendment Act), Amendments to the criminal law which made crime against women a punishable offence.

Many initiatives were also carried out in various Five Year Plans to maximise the participation of women in different development programmes. For the first time a chapter on "Women and Development" was included in the Sixth Five year Plan, introducing women specific and related programmes which can bring improvement in the socio-economic condition of women. Further the Eight Five Year Plan introduced a variety of development programmes specifically for women. Under the National Perspective Plan for women provision was made to maximise the participation of women in on going IRDP and other programmes introduced at providing self-employment opportunities. During this plan, an Indira Mahila Yojana was introduced, and a Rastriya Mahila Kosh established to encourage women to hold their own saving's accounts and funds for productive activities.

The outcome of these measures undertaken in different plans for the upliftment of women's status and socio-economic condition, have certainly attracted to women to associate and participate in different development programmes. However, lack of awareness among a large segment of rural women living in backward and remote areas under the subjugation of men, social and cultural boundations restricting them to remain within the household etc. has limited the actual participation of women to a lower level.

Observing the performance and achievement level of past planning strategies and policies initiated for improving the status and empowering women the debates had been widely spread out among the policy makers and socials reformers about how women could be empowered in the presently existing social backwardness and traditional restrictions imposed in rural hierarchical system against women. It was, therefore, emphasised that the solution for empowering women could rest in the situation of their political partnership. Political partnership can be considered to include an involvement in any form of organised activity that seeks to influence the attitudes and behaviour of those who have power of decision making. But it is also universally believed, considering the past experiences, that the efforts undertaken for empowerment of women suffered due to nexus of traditional factors of castes, class, religion, feudal and family status which are essentially patriarchal forces that work in favour of men against women. Even in voting for any election the rights of women for voting are restricted resulting that their turnout is much less than men due to pressure from family and society. Equally important factor in this regard is lack of awareness among women regarding the importance and rights of their casting votes.

Women in Panchayati Raj System

With the objective of maximising the participation of women in public mainstream, political system and decision making process is seen clearly in the changes incorporated in the Panchayati Raj System. The objective of bringing improvement in the socio-economic condition of women could be successful only by taking suitable initiatives and measures for empowering them. Women cannot be empowered unless they are provided proper representation in the political system. This objective is understood to be achieved at desired level through making the provision of linking and associating maximum number of women in political affairs even at the lowest level of political activity.

In the recently introduced Panchayati Raj System, the policy for reservation in favour of women has, therefore, been thought as an important approach to maximise their participation in the local level political system and decision making process in the activities of rural areas. Under the 73rd amendment of constitution ofPanchayati Raj System, one third of the total seats of members and heads of village Panchayat, Block Panchayat and District Panchayat are reserved for women candidates. Conceptually, providing representation to women in Panchayati Raj System could be accepted as an important planning approach regarding minimising the traditional feelings of people about the status of women in our society, particularly in terms of keeping women under the subjugation of men, imposing restrictions by the households and society against them in the availment of certain opportunities and several other social, cultural and traditional boundations disfavouring them for improving personal life style and status in existing social and economic setting.

Consequently this newly introduced policy would enhance the possibilities of increasing equalities in the process of socio-economic development, participation in different activities in mutual understandings, status and role to pay in the household and the activities performed outside households and different decision making processes of the family among men and women. This would also develop the understanding of women regarding their duties and rights about national welfare and its integrity and they will be able to contribute effectively along with their male counterparts. However, the achievement level of these intervention undertaken by the Government to safeguard the interest and provide empowerment to women would more especially depend upon its implementation process an flexibility maintained in its implementation criteria based on regional! area specific social and cultural elements and conditions, level of awareness of the realities an objectives of the policy to different socio-economic groups of women. Beside this, the factors such as educational level, local environmental situation, attitude of family particularly its male members, past background of women related to the pattern of their participation in different social, political and related activities, category and groups of women elected as the representatives of Panchayats at its different tiers, socio-economic status and background and several other factors are equally important elements of achieving the level of success of the introduced policy intervention.

RESERVATION POLICY

It is believed that planning initiatives for achieving the goal of increasing participation of women through the recently introduced Panchayati Raj System could be an important instrument measure for empowering women and bringing desirable improvements in their socio-economic and political status. In this regard the policy of reservation of one third seats for women in village, block and district level panchayats was introduced. The provisions were also made to strengthen the Panchayati Raj institutions by providing various administrative rights and duties, financial powers and the freedom to make initiatives for generating finances locally from different sources.

Implementation Process

The anouncement of the implementation of Panchayati Raj System in Uttarakhand was carried out during November 1996. And, it took about two months in the identification and fixation of criteria for the reservation of seats for women in the three tier system of Panchayats and the finalisation of various formalities for the implementation of the Panchayati Raj System. The village development officer was designated as a responsible person for the fixation and identification of village Panchayats, implementation of criteria fixed for reserving certain village Panchayats for women Pradhan, number of seats to be reserved for women members in each village Panchayats etc.

Thus the election of the Pradhans and members of village Panchayats were held by the end of December 1996. Implementation of Panchayati Raj System in Uttarakhand started with the preparation of house listing of every village. In most ofthe cases existing Gram Sabhas were converted into a village Panchayat. However, there were larger numbers of village Sabhas having small size of population and were earlier provided the status of Gram Sabha due to the existing geographical and topographical problems in their locational settings, the village panchayats were formed by merging two or more such small village sabhas into single village Panchayat. In the initiation of such procedure the option was left open for the inhabitants of concerned villages to suggest and provide collective choice and preference about the merger of their villages. Beside this, the locational aspects related to the geographical and topographical situation of identified villages was also considered as an important element for the merger of villages in forming village panchayats. For the purpose of the implementation of reservation policy for favour of women firstly, all the village panchayats were listed in alphabatical order and secondly, 34 village panchayats m that alphabetical order were made reserved for women Pradhan in each Block Panchayat.

Later the location-wise categorisation of households into 9 to 11 groups was undertaken in each village panchayats for the purpose of the fixation of the constituency of the members of panchayat. In each village panchayat 3 to 4 constituencies were, thus, kept reserved for women candidates. When people at the village level were informed that the proposed village panchayats will be provided larger financial resources and additional administrative powers the election took place in almost all the village panchayats for both village pradhans as well as its members.

This emerging political environment has given birth to groupism, social clashes and conflicts. As a consequence traditionally maintained co-operation and friendly environment among different groups of population has begun to deteriorate. In fact, several groups emerged and the households were divided into various groups and division during the election periods. However, once the process of formation of panchayats was completed the general public as well as the representatives of the village panchayats found that no new benefits were appearing in the introduction of this revised Panchayati Raj System. So the traditional system of cooperation and friendly environment have started redeveloping in various villages. Only a major change was reported by the local people in terms of providing representation to women in the new form of Panchayats; though a significant number of male population has shown dissatisfaction over the introduction of reservation policy in favour of women.

Local Perceptions for Empowering Women

(a) **Status and Women.** The women have been regarded as a backbone of the region in terms of the role they have been playing in the development and prosperity of the Uttarakhand for he past several generations. However, in most of the cases they lack equal treatment, behaviour and status as provided to their male counterparts. They have been participating in different activities at household and outside household level along with male members of the family. In fact certain activities are performed only by the women at household level.

(b) **Participatory Role.** Moreover, the domination of women in population, workforce, local environment and economic development process is quite evident in almost the entire mountain areas of the region. The close association of women, directly or indirectly, with different activities at household, social, cultural, community and regional levels has been a long history in the tradition of area specific socio-cultural system. This deep rooted association and linkages of women with local social and cultural environment had been a channel of encouragemet for maintaining the traditional value system and ideology of the region. The system of co-operation and friendly atmosphere in the behaviour of mountain people prevailing has been maintained without any hesitation and without any basic shortcoming for the past several generations. Even in currently increasing situation of socio-economic conflicts among local masses influenced by the

forces outside uttarakhand, is also only a short term phenomenon and the women folk are engrossed in a battle against this evil and should be able to overcome the situation without much problem.

In most areas of Uttarakhand the women are well aware about their basic responsibilities, duties and the way they can devote their energies in the interest and welfare of the region. In this context the mass participation of women in various social movements organised for imposition of ban on the opening of wine shops in the region, environmental and economic movements, widely known as chipko movement against increasing deforestration and degradation of mountain environment, and on going political movement in favour of creation of separate Uttarakhand state are some examples which prove the awareness among women.

The reasons and factors associated with motivating active participation of women in different socio-economic and political movements in the past have been the rise of those activities, which have gone against the interest of women largely. They have felt that the increasing rise and development of such activities which were carried out under protection of local unsocial elements for their self interest and the unability of Government to interven and impose ban on those activities would ultimately create problems in the peaceful socio-economic and environmental setting of the region; also they would be the main sufferers if development of such undesirable activities is carried out. For instance the cause of mass participation of women in Chipko movement has been the result of excessive and increasing deforestration by the forest mafias and contractors belonging both to Uttarakhand and outside Uttarakhand mismanagement of forest department, lack of intervention on the part of Government to impose ban on over exploitation of various forest products. The influencial local men and contractors have also started participating with the forest mafias in deforestation merely for obtaining short-term financial gains. In the mean time, women had realised that the increasing deforestation would create serious problem for them in obtaining fodder for animals, fuelwood for cooking and heating, timber for house construction and different forest products for various purposes. The ultimate sufferer of deforestration would be women because the collection of forest products is the responsibility and prime duty of women. As a result women have established various women societies and organisations to fight against deforestration and they have succeeded to a considerable extent in their efforts.

Similarly, lack of introducing developing planning according to the acceptability of local geographical, topographical and related local conditions and thus marginalisation of the region in planning for development resulting in increasing un-employment, increasing dependency of Government upon the natural resources of the region for satisfying the demands of outside region without providing any incentive and development gains to the local areas in exchange of exploiting area specific local resources have motivated the women volunteers to organise collectively for demanding separate statehood of Uttarakhand.

Agitation of women for imposition of ban on the supply of wine and other alcoholic products is another most popular movement initiated in almost all mountain areas of the region during eighties. This movement had been successful in achieving its goal in 1977 when the Government had restricted the use and supply of wine and related items in the region, though local mafias and businessmen had started supplying alcoholic products in the name of ayurvedic medicines. This issue was brought into notice of judiciary by the women organisations and a ban was imposed on the sale of these alcoholic products. Again the women's movement received mass co-operation and assistance from students, N.G.O.'s and various social workers in 1991-92 when the Government had permitted the wine contractors to open wine shops even at tehsil level and in small towns. The movement of women against opening wine shops on mass scale is an ongoing process with the slogan of *Nasha Nahi Rajagar Doe* In this regard the women volunteers are well supported and influenced by the national level women's organisations to carry out agitations with maximising the participation of women. The participation of women has been very appreciable in the local level agitations and movements organised for bringing improvement and change in the socio-economic conditions of women and general development of the region in the past.

The most important factors behind the mass level participation of women in different movements could be the domination of women in different activities, maintaining traditional social systems and cultural values, more responsibilities as compared to men in performing household related activities, high incidence of male migration resulting in a majority, of households being headed by women and relatively higher literacy rates of women in the region as compared to state and national level.

Possibility of Empowering Women

Considering the involvement and domination of women in different activities, historical experiences regarding their participation in various regional movements associated to different moves, level and pattern of awareness about the regional development and maintaining traditional value system and having relatively better educational attainment it is expected that the introduction of Panchayati Raj System and reservation policy for women in the Panchayat could be an important instrumental measure for achieving improvements in the socio-economic status and strengthening the empowerment of women in Uttarakhand. Moreover, the policy and planning for empowering women could be more successful in Uttarakhand as compared to other areas and states in view of the higher literacy, better awareness and active participation in the local level movements in the region.

However, the motive of policy introduction on empowering women would mainly depend upon its implementing process, socio-economic and political background and characteristics of elected women representatives in the village Panchayats. Factors such as the attitude and intention of elected womens towards the initiation of various development programms and the capacity in making efforts to link different segment of village population with the introduced programms also matter very much in improving the status of women representatives in the social environment of the village Panchayat.

Identification of Reserved Village Panchayats

The procedure for identification and fixation of locations as reserved for women candidates adopted at village panchayat level have already been highlighted. However, the time devoted in identification of reserved village panchayats for women pradhans and reserved locations/constituencies for its women members was very short. Limited duration of two months between the announcement of election and the actual dates fixed for final election had limited the scope of a large number of women having relatively better socio-economic and political background, better educational level and social outlook as compared to most women elected as members and the pradhans in the various village panchayats. It would have been more appropriate to initiate the measures for providing knowledge and awareness among villagers in general and women in particular about the reservation of seats for different sex and social groups of population in different village panchayats so that most eligible women candidates would have found the opportunity of contesting election for these positions.

A majority of the identified villages brought under the reservation for women pradhans had the representation of well educated women. Some of the women in few villages had even participated in social movements organised at regional level in the past. However, in certain villages the well educated women could not contest election either for the post of Pradhan or members of the village panchayats because of restrictions imposed by their heads of households due to higher work load, social backwardness, lack of awareness about the duties, benefits and role of elected women in the Panchayats, etc. Procedures adopted for the fixation of reservation of seats for women in the Panchayats and identification of village Panchayats as reserved for women candidates was not based on the local condition of geographical and topographical settings of villages but it was base on the same pattern or criteria as adopted in the plain areas of the state. Seneral viilage Panchayats, which were identified for reservation of women Pradhan are located in remote, inaccessible and away from the nearest road heads and block headquarter. This has been creating a serious problem to women pradhan to participate in meetings regularly which are organised outside their respective villages and at block office. On an average, reaching the block office from some of the respective village panchayats takes more than one day.

In the process of identification of village panchayats for implementing reservation policy for women candidates the locational aspects of concerned villages in terms of topographical, geographical and accessibility situation should have been given top priority. This was the beginning of implementing a new policy and introduction of any new policy basically requires maximum support and participation of local people. Care should also have been taken to include flexibility options based on locally acceptable conditions and prevailing situations for the successful implementation of the concerned programme. So, selection of village panchayats located in better accessible areas and neighbouring to block headquarter for reservation of women Pradhan would have been a important element in maximising the participation of women Pradhans in different meetings held outside their respective village Panchayats.

Similarly, the procedure adopted for the identification of reserved village Panchayats for women Pradhans and locations/areas within the village panchayats for women members should have provided greater opportunity to the well educated women and to those having higher contribution in the various regional movements and local level social reform activities as compared to the women who have actually availed the opportunity to find place in the village Panchayats and Pradhan and the members.

●●●

8

Women and Decision-making

There are very few studies on the internal dynamics of the Indian family, specifically decision-making process. One classic study in the area is by Gore who studied samples of Aggarwal families around Delhi. In his book *"Urbanisation and Family Change"*, Gore has devoted one chapter on "Decision-making in the Family", based on this study. Among questions considered were who plays a major role in important decisions like schooling, occupation, mate-selection, perception of decision-making, and ruralurban differences. Gore's findings are not every different from those of Khatri *viz.*, eldest male plays a very significant role but he does consult other relatives including his spouse in important areas like mate-selection; there is considerable involvement of kin in important decisions. Chekki has also described the process of decision-making, and the extent to which respondents were consulted and relatives to whom they consulted while making important decisions. Matrilateral kin and affines played significant role. He refers to decline of authority of the eldest male under the impact of modernisation.

Socialisation Personality and Decision-making

It is postulated here that ability to make decisions of seeking active involvement in the decision-making process is linked with personality. Personality with high dependency strivings, with high 'succorant' needs, to use Murray's conceptualisation, incapacitates the person in making important decisions, and contributes towards reluctance and hesitancy which prevents him/her from seeking out an active role in the decision-making process when more than one person are engaged in the process of decision-making.

It is hypothesised here that individuals socialised in the traditional joint family environment in India are likely to devel9P basic personality structure which is characterised by dependence, reduced drive for initiative innovative orientation and creativity. These personality characteristics are quite relevant for making decisions of playing an active role in the decision-making process.

It is assumed here that child-rearing environment in general and child-rearing practices in particular provide a basic framework for certain dispositions, unconscious assumptions, basic expectancy sets, broad attitudes of relating to persons in general and to certain role occupants in particular. According to Kardiner and Linton, a definite groundwork is laid for the basic personality structure by common child rearing methods in a given culture. We will begin by consideration of socialisation of the Hindu male in joint family. He is exposed to a family atmosphere that is traditionally authoritarian, demanding obdience to family elders and conformity to the family's rules and regulations.

He begins to experience a variety of disciplining agents; he is given immediate negative reinforcement for familydisapproved behaviour, and this is further reinforced when he is witness to the system of negative reinforcement operating in the case of other children. Repeated exposures of this sort are likely to generate a strong sense of conformity and provide the basis for anxiety reactions to nonconformity. The authoritarian family climate encourages dependence and passivity and stifles the strivings for autonomy. Firmly embedded conformity and built-in anxiety about nonconformity become additional barriers to the emergence of independence and creative activity. Industrialisation in India creates problems for such a Hindu male. Let us envisage the following situation. Having been to college, the highly educated Hindu youth socialised in the joint family secures a responsible executive position in an organisation. This position, however, demands initiative, independence of thinking and of decision-making for which he is psychologically unprepared due to his basic personality structure characterised by dependence. This inability on the part of the Hindu youth to fulfill the requirements of modern society has been described by the author as "personality lag," which may also have repercussions on the mental health of the individual. Space consideration prevents us from dealing with socialisation of the Hindu female, which is in many ways similar and is linked with her personality and decision-making. Extensive discussion of links between personality of the Hindu male and female and familial socialisation as well as impact of social change on these links can be found elsewhere.

EMPIRICAL STUDIES OF DECISION-MAKING

Parental Preference Study

This study by Khatri was a replication of Hartley's similar study on American children. It has been assumed that the socialisation process in the American as well as Indian family, which conveys explicitly and implicitly patriarchal values and attitudes, prompt children *(a)* to perceive males as the preferred sex invested with power and prestige; *(b)* to identify with it; and *(c)* to reflect these perceptions and attitudes in their expressed preferences. The sample in the Parental Study consisted of 147 children from two schools in Ahmedabad—an industrial city in Western India. Their socio-economic status evaluated with the aid of Kuppuswami's scale was predominantly upper and middle class.

The following groups contituted the sample: *(a)* 39 eight year old boys, *(b)* 40 eight year old girls, *(c)* 37 eleven year old girls. In an individual interview (conducted in the regional Gujarati language), each child was asked to complete a story of a couple intending to adopt a child. The child was asked to answer the following questions, along with others: (1) "Which do you think they chose?" (2) "Which do you think the husband wanted?" (3) "Which do you think the wife wanted?" (4) "Why do you think they chose?" This analysis confirmed Hartley's finding of no generalised partiality for either sex of the offspring and parallel sex preferences (*i.e.,* father preferring a boy, mother preferring a girl) of the father, but not of the mother.

In the second phase of the Parental Preference Study, analysis was done on responses of children to questions one and four above. This analysis was carried to the stage of an agreed-upon choice, not what father figure or mother figure individually preferred but whom (a boy or a girl) they adopted. The study revealed the following findings: (1) 71.43 percent of the total sample attributed to story parent agreed-upon preference for a boy in response to question one; (2) Age also contributed to variability in perceptions so far as eleven year old female subjects were concerned. Preferences for the boy are prompted by functional (*e.g.* economic support) rather affectional considerations.

Jointness Scale Development Study

A sample of 118 adult respondents from families of children studying in two schools was interviewed to provide relevant data for development of a scale to measure jointness of families in India. Age range of children was from 2 years to 14 years 8 months. Mean age of children about whose family information was collected was 7 years. Socio-economic status of families of children from one school was upper class (I) and upper middle class (II) while it was upper middle and low middle (III) of another school, as measured by Kuppuswami's Scale. Findings of analysis of a part of the data concerning decision-making and extent of consultation among kin are: (1) That family head had decided on his own in very few cases. (2) In one out of three cases, the family head consulted with his wife or relatives. (3) In resident nuclear families, husbands and wives consulted each other more often than in other family types. (4) Non-residential kin were involved in decision-making in considerable number of cases.

Cross-cultural Family Relations Study

This study by Khatri inter alia, aimed at various dimensions of decision-making *viz.*, patterns of decision-making, (autocratic, autonomous, dyadic, democratic), the extent of consultation sought by and from families of respondents and relatives not living with them, and the major role played by relatives-residential (living with the respondent) and non-residential (living with the respondent). Only one dimension of decision-making *viz.*, and major role played by relatives is reported here.

The sample consisted of students taking various courses offered by school of social and Behavioural Sciences, University College, University of Alabama at Birmingham and also students from colleges in South and Western India. Analysis on which this study is based is. derived from coded and computer-processed schedules of 574 American (474 white and 100 black) students and 580 East Indian students who answered a question: "Who would you say plays a major role when important decisions are made in your family?" Examples of important decisions given to American respondents were: choice of education, business, purchase of car, a colour T.V., a house, etc.; for Indian respondents, marriage of a family member and choice of a marriage partner replaced examples of purchase of car and colour T.V. A semi-structured interview was used in the initial phase of the study while a questionnaire eliciting similar information was developed to provide easier and extended coverage of groups of students. The highest frequency of students stayed in the family type, nuclear parental; hence data on decision-making (who plays a major role) on this type were included. In both the American and Indian samples, father of the respondent is reported with largest frequency (36.53% of American and 70.00% of the Indian students). The Indian father plays a major role in significantly more families than does his American counterpart. Percentage of mothers playing a major role in both American and East Indian samples is much less than that by the father but more than each of other specified relatives (19.69%, American 16.55%, Indian). There are no significant cultural differences in the attribution of a major role to the mother in American and Indian samples.

Heterosexual Friendship Study

The study by Khatri, hints at some aspects of socialisation climate of family-reared adults. It explores "Heterosexual Friendships and Involvempnt in Mate Selection Process of Primary and Secondary Teacher Traineess in Ahmedabad." Criteria for the sample were as follow: (1) all respondents, must be Hindus; (2) all of them must be males; and (3) all of them must be either married or betrothed.

Social Novels Content Analysis Study

The study aims at gaining into dynamic processes and inner intra-personality states of characters involved in heterosexual relations engagement, marriage and divorce family relationships (*e.g.*, conjugal, relationships in the family of orientation and in-laws) and social change in these as reflected in 45 Gujarati social novels. Among dimensions investigated was: decision-making process in family-arranged betrothals and self-selected betrothals. A category system of

143 items and 699 sub-items was developed which, interlia, explored the decision-making process. Among the findings were: (1) Father stood out significantly as a major decision-making individual, (2) In a significant number of cases, mother and other relatives were consulted by the father, (3) In a few cases, preview, of potential mate was arranged for seeking reaction of mate concerned, (4) Major social change was from family arrangements of betrothal at an early age of mates, preteen to teen age without any involvement of mates to consultation of mature mates especially in recent urban novels. In most self-selected betrothals, a decision to marry was arrived at in one of the following ways: (1) by exposure to admiration of a potential mate without seeing him, (2) just seeing a potential mate from distance without interacting: with him, (3) meeting once only, usually in a "damsel in distress" situation in which a brave male saved a helpless female, (4) prolonged interaction leading to development of bilateral heterosexual love.

Discussion

What is necessary is undertaking of empirical researches exploring diverse dimensions of model, usually (overt), and basic (covert) personality structure through a variety of research techniques like the Jointness Scale, projective tests, interviews, systematic observation in small groups, (specially of executives in important decision-making situations), on samples of joint-family reared and nuclear-family-reared individuals in India as well as comparable samples in other cultures. The Parental Preference Study hints at certain significant elements in the socialisation process of these predominantly middle and upper class children. Preference for the male sex was confirmed by this study. Boys in the sample seem to have internalised this preference for male sex in patriarchally oriented Indian culture; they have made it egosyntonic and expressed it in their pattern of preference.

Girls tend to do the same thought in somewhat attenuated form. Internalisation of the high evaluation of the male appears to have developed with increasing age, older children internalising it much more than the younger group. Reasons for male preference also shed some light on the socialisation climate of Indian families: a boy supporting parents in old age, bringing a wife who can help and similar reasons given by eight year old and eleven year old children reflects internalisation of joint family orientation in their process of growing up. The exact process of internalisation, the role of direct didactic demands and commands, exposure to role models in families and extra-familial day-to-day life, reinforcement of this learning in religious literature (exposure to role models in great epics, *Ramayana, Mahabharat* and other scriptures and sacred books), identification with parents and therefore their values, subtle socialisation pressures operating in the school environment the extent of impact of all these socialisation in Indian families. In the Jointness Scale Development Study, in very few families we find the traditional pattern of pater families deciding on his own, without consulting anyone. In about one out of three families, the family head consults with either his wife or other relatives. In residentially nuclear families, husbands and wives consulted with each other more often than in other family types. Non-residential kins were involved in decision-making in considerable number of cases.

In one out often cases, almost the whole family becomes involved in decision-making. For those who have hypothesised an increase in individual patterns, these findings are disappointing as in only one case, did the party concerned decide without consulting the family head or any other family members. When we analyse the data concerning pattern of decision-making adopted in the case of thirty-nine engagement marriages, we find that only in three cases the party concerned made an autonomous decision about a matter of great importance in his life. Children are likely to observe the decision-making process in their household. Role of decision-making as providing linkage between families, as an index of nature and extent of kin involvement also deserves study in its own right. This has been done in the Cross-cultural Family Relations Study as well as the Scale Development Study. Another area from which we can gain insight into decision-making in families is the rather extensively studied area of small groups from social psychological perspective.

Cross-fertilisation of social psychology of small groups and family sociology can yeild rich insights into our understanding of decision-making in families. The social Novels Content Analysis Study sheds elements of light on intra-familial interaction involved in family-arranged betrothals and heterosexual dyadic interaction in self-selected betrothals. A major limitation of the study is that fiction does not correspond with reality on one-to-one basis. Authors exaggerate certain aspects and ignore significant sectors of social reality. One common finding of most of studies on decision-making reported here is abundant evidence of patriarchal Indian family in contemporary India. The family organisation is Characterised by male dominance in decision-making, desirability of the male offspring and considerable kin interaction and involvement in decision-making. As will be seen, studies of decisionmaking in the Indian family undertaken by the author and some other investigators have explored just a few components of the "universe" of the concept, "decision-making." Among components of this "universe" are: who makes in what groups, in conjugal dyads, in nuclear, broken and other family types, areas in which decisions are made, patterns of decision-making (nature of authority and involvement, *e.g.*, autocratic, democratic), as interactional process, outcomes of decision-making, relationship of decision-making to traditional *vs.* emerging sex roles. A few comments reflecting global evaluation of the work in the area of decision-making may not be considered out of place here.

- Very little empirical research has been undertaken on the decision-making process in the Indian family. Adoption of a variety of research techniques and diverse samples along with operational definitions and repeated replications of these studies are essential to arrive at the common core of verified findings in this important area of research.
- It is needless to point out the importance of cross-national research in sociology in general and in the specific areas of socialisation, personality and decision-making. Special problems encountered by the present author in his cross-cultural researches as well as those of other workers are found in the area of conceptual equilivance and phenomenal identity.
- A practical suggestion for family sociologists in universities and research institutes is to encourage replication of studies by graduate students with the same vigour that they (family sociologists) encourage innotative investigations.

●●●

9

Women's Organisation and Empowerment

It is generally admitted that the participation is determined by the socio-economic status of the members and office bearers of Mahila Mandals. In other words, it is hypothesised that higher the socio-economic status of the functionaries of Mandals higher will be their participation in the programme. The explanation to the socio-economic status of the people working in Mahila Mandals depends on a large number of inter-related qualitative and quantitative factors.

An attempt was also made to find out the nature and extent of their participation in the programme. The salient features of the trends emerging out of these sections are summarised in the following paragraphs. The cultural roots of eastern and western Uttar Pradesh extend into the antiquity now constitutes one of the poorest and richest peripheral regions of the state. The district Varanasi is placed on both sides of the Ganga river whereas Ghaziabad is lying in between the rivers Ganga and Yamuna called 'Doab' region. The economy of both the districts is dominated by agriculture which together with the allied activities forms the most important source of employment and revenue.

The growth of population is higher in Ghaziabad as compared to Varanasi over the decade 1981-91. In case of literacy, Ghaziabad was better placed. In both the districts, people were mainly engaged in agriculture and allied activities. As regards infrastructural facilities, the district of Ghaziabad is highly developed both agriculturally and industrially and also serves as a hinterland of Delhi metropolis. On the other hand, the Varanasi district is a large town characterized by its traditional character and devoid of development in any major field.

As regards ICDS coverage, a total of six blocks in Varanasi are covered under the scheme. Whereas in Ghaziabad the scheme is being implemented in only three blocks. Even the children beneficiaries were covered more in Varanasi as compared to Ghaziabad. However, in case of mothers (both pregnant and lactating), the situation was just reverse. All the project level staff was in position against their sanctioned strength in both the projects. However, three and two posts of Supervisors in Bhojpur and Chakia were respectively vacant. The vacant posts of Anganwadi Workers were as high as 31 in Bhojpur and only two in Chakia. The requirement of trained manpower had received due importance in the area under study.

Most of the Supervisors of both the projects were from the socially backward community. This was, however, not true in the case of Anganwadi Workers. Educationally as well as experience-wise workers of Bhojpur were better as compared to that of Chakia and by and large, projects and AWCs were well equipped.

All the services of ICDS scheme were being delivered satisfactorily except HNE and referral services. Supervision by the project and field level staff was also according to the prescribed norms. Field level functionaries had made frequent visits to the Centres. As regards coordination, it was lacking at the grassroots level but adequate at the project level. MPW (Female) were not coordinating very well for the health components with the Anganwadi Workers.

In both the districts there is very little coordination between the agencies/departments concerned with Mahila Mandals. The Executive Committees were expected to manage mandal's activities in accordance with the overall policy guidance provided by the General Body. The extent of participation of the members in the meetings do not appear to be important from the point of view of their real contribution to development/welfare activities. By and large, main activities performed by the Mandals/Women Groups were to educate women and children, look after the malnourished children and women, help in cooking and distribution of supplementary nutrition and in organising pre-school activities.

A majority of the members belonged to lower stratum of the society. The involvement of women from weaker section was relatively low. Educational achievements of the members were also very low. Most of the members were doing the Mandal's work as their secondary occupation on both the districts.

As the ICDS Scheme in the area under study has been in operation for more than seven years, the villagers were well acquainted with its different components. All the sample households had sufficient knowledge about the programme. The first source of information about the scheme in a majority of the cases were Anganwadi workers and it has been observed that the socio-economic conditions of the sample beneficiaries was akin to that of total beneficiaries in the area under study. By and large, the scheduled castes and other backward castes were receiving the services of ICDS in the same magnitude as others. The family size of the sample beneficiaries and non-beneficiaries more or less confirms with the national assumption that in the rural areas. The age structure was biased towards young. Among the two selected blocks, literacy level of the beneficiaries was better in Bhojpur of Ghaziabad district as compared to Chakia (Varanasi).

However, most of the illiterates and those studied up to the primary were also took active part in the scheme.

Bhojpur being an industrial region attracted more people for service, as a result most of the households were having service as their main occupation. While in Chakia a majority of the households were engaged in agriculture and allied work. Because of this occupational differences, the beneficiaries and non-beneficiaries of Bhojpur were well-off in terms of income standard.

It was observed in both the blocks that the community participation is not upto the mark. It is therefore, attitudinal change on the part of the community as well as bureaucracy is required. On the other hand, the concept of integrated services should be taken into account for institutional arrangements. At least the functionaries of the two streams namely; the health and ICDS set-up should work in close cooperation with each other in a coordinated manner. All the required efforts for achieving this must come from the personnel of both the systems, feasible mechanisms for promoting interactions and vertical horizontal linkages must be identified and institutionalised.

Based on the statistical analysis, the extent of participation and effective involvement of Mahila Mandals in the ICDS scheme has been worked out. The participation is determined by the socio-economic status of the members and office bearers of Mahila Mandals. The representation of the lower stratum of the society was not proportionate to their numerical strength in the concerned villages of both the projects. This is because of the fact that women belonging to these sections did not find any thing that might help them in their economic or domestic problems. In other words, the activities of the Mandals were having limited appeal to these sections. Secondly, a majority of the Mandals were located in the houses of one of the office bearers or members belonging to higher status, and hence, they did not feel free to visit these houses because of prevailing social inhibitions. A majority of the Mandals of Bhojpur (Ghaziabad) take active part in providing support to Anganwadi Workers, participating in AWC activities, coordinating with AWWs and publicising the programme. In rest of the activities their participation were marginal. As regards effective involvement, most of the Mandals devoted one to two hours daily, providing drinking water and fuel at the Anganwadi Centre in Bhojpur (Ghaziabad). While in Chakia (Varanasi), besides these services they also help Anganwadi Workers in getting space for the Centre, ration and equipment.

It has been observed that the major contributing factors in participation and effective involvement of Mandals were lack of regional advancement, remote location, lack of support of the functionaries and poor socio-cultural and economic conditions of the members and office bearers of Mandal. The results of composite index reveals that Mandals ofChakia participate more in the programme as compared to Bhojpur but their involvement was less than that of Chakia. By and large, the contribution of Mahila Mandals have made to improving the services of ICDS on the one hand and in the overall task of women's and rural development on the other. This is evident from the fact that the activities were invariably, printed towards welfare programme.

CONCLUSIONS

General

Most of the families in the area under study depended on agriculture for their sustenance. Safe drinking water was accessible to all the households in both the projects. Social convenience like, media, social clubs, electricity, educational facilities etc. were observed to be better in Bhojpur as compared to Chakia.

Related to Public Health

The study has brought out great neglect in the area of health services particularly health and nutrition education and referral services. It has been observed that these two services for which provision has been made in the scheme remained almost unattended in the area under study.

It has been observed that in all pre and post natal activities associated with the child birth, including the actual delivery of the child, the involvement of the public health manpower provided in the blocks has been very marginal. Evidences clearly bring out the need for radical, review of approach to public health delivery system in the rural areas.

Related to ICDS

In general, AWCs lacked the basic amenities need for efficient functioning of the scheme as mostly centres were functioning in one roomed thatched structures without proper ventilation and adequate space. However, Anganwadi Centres of Bhojpur were better placed as compared to Chakia.

The coverage of children under immunization was better in Bhojpur as compared to Chakia but much below the level envisaged under UP.

Among the different services of ICDS scheme, supplementary nutrition seemed to be most popular. The food was usually distributed with a standardised spoon or cup/mug and hence, the children often received similar quantities of supplement irrespective of their age or nutritional grade. Most of the children consumed the nutrition at the centre whereas women beneficiaries preferred to carry it home:

The workers rarely used the growth chart as a visual tool for explaining the child's growth process and educating the mothers. The drugs supplied to workers were grossly inadequate.

The attitude and perception of the 'providers' in general was favourable towards the programme on the one hand whereas on the other 'consumers' generally perceived ICDS as a programme meant for welfare of women and children. However, non-availability of the worker, in accessibility of centre, inconvenient time of distributing the supplement were some of the complaints.

It was observed that some of the community members played positive role in providing suitable accommodation for locating the centre and motivating women to utilize ICDS services. Though the mothers were happy with the non-formal pre-school education, but also insisted on formal method of teaching alphabets number etc.

Although the scheme succeeded in providing a grassroot worker at village level with a mandate to provide health, nutrition and educational services in an integrated manner with a focus on mother and child. However, the operational constraints and lack of effective coordination between health and programme functionaries and differing perceptions among consumers and provides seem to be some of the weaknesses in the programme which need strengthening, The envisaged convergence of programmes of providing safe drinking water, improved environment and communication facilities to the ICDS block is not much in evidence.

It was observed in both the blocks that the community participation in scheme is not upto the mark. Thus, attitudinal change on the part of the community as well as bureaucracy is required.

RELATED TO MAHILA MANDAL

It was observed that the Mandals were generally working on an informal basis without observing systematic procedures in their organisational management, in holding meetings etc. The functions of the office-bearers were not clearly laid down and the work of the Mandals was being carried out by some selected enthusiastic persons.

A few women from the concerned villages had enrolled themselves as members of these organisations, indicating thereby that they have not succeeded in bringing into their fold a majority of the population.

The study revealed that the leadership in a majority of the Mandals was confined to those belonging to high castes, and members from weaker sections were not adequately represented in them in spite of the fact that they accounted for a considerable proportion of the total membership. In general, the Mandals did not have any regular source of income and, as a result, their working depended either on grants or on donations from the villagers. On the other hand, there were some Mandals, which had no income whatsoever. Only a few were able to raise their own resources by undertaking some economic projects. With few exceptions, these activities were, by and large meagre. As a result, the Mandals were left with no funds to undertake incomegenerating projects, which could attract women from the weaker sections.

One of the main reasons for poor performance of the Mandals was the non-availability of infra structural facilities such as office accommodation. It was found that Mandals were endowed with their own accommodation.

Main activities performed by the Mandals/Women Groups were, to educate women and children, look after the malnourished children and women, help in cooking and distribution of supplementary nutrition and in organising pre-school activities. It was found that wherever official guidance was available, the Mandals/Groups were able to carry out the activities successfully.

Lack of fund, buildings, activities suiting to the socioeconomic background of the members, supervision and technical guidance, clear understanding of the objectives were reported to be the main factors inhibiting the working of the Mandals. Most of the members of the Mandals tended to prefer those programmes through which they can speed their spare time. However, the contribution of these organisations have made to improving the functioning of Anganwadi Centres on the one hand, and in the overall task of Anganwadi workers on the other, has been found to be some extent.

It is too much to expect the Mandals to show any work without any financial base. This could possibly be done either by enthusing them to mobilize resources locally or by providing them with grants-in-aid on a regular basis.

Despite the shortcomings, the Mandals have played an important role in making the rural women to come out of their homes and intereact with the forces of modernisation in terms of participation in community affairs besides elevating their own social status. These have also provided in them a measure of social confidence while dealing with officials and non-officials working at the block and the village levels.

There cannot be a better medium for the development of skills of the traditional women than these organisations, which can promote their participation in economic, social and political spheres. It is therefore, the entire effort in respect of developing Mahila Mandals has to be viewed from the perspective of human resource development. Whatever investment is made in the promotion of these organisations will ultimately prove to be a sound investment in human capital.

Recommendation

An integrated approach to attempt for human development *viz.* women and child development required that all aspects of social and economic life of the community to be brought within the purview of the framework of effort designed and fabricated for the purpose. However, some relevant policy implications emerging from the study are recommended as follows:

The findings of the study have drawn attention to some aspects of ICDS, which need to considered for smooth functioning of the scheme. A few such recommendations are given below:

(i) The present reporting system of ICDS monitoring should include information on local village level organizations as well in detail. In order to make everything more effective, relevant information should also be integrated at one place to give a holistic picture of ICDS implementation.

(ii) Provision of suitable building either through rural development programme like, Jawahar Rozgar Yojana, IRDP, MNP or local organisation for housing the Anganwadi Centres should be given priority. This should have adequate indoor and outdoor space to carry out the regular activities like, non-formal pre-school education, health and nutrition education sessions etc.

(iii) The study has identified two basic reasons for the inadequate success in the delivery of public health services in the rural areas. The first is the manpower composition of the organization of current health services, which is grossly biased in favour of specialist on the curative side. The second has been the putting together under one organization of two activities which in terms of their input requirements, delivery technology and focus of activity are not integrable. It is therefore, suggested that atleast one medical

Officer should also be posted at the PHC level from public health background.

(iv) The Multipurpose workers both male and female should be familiar with the concepts and components of IGDS scheme. They should be well acquainted of their role in integrating health components to the ongoing nutrition and HNE activities carried out by the Anganwadi Workers. It is suggested that all about ICDS programme should be taught to the health functionaries during their professional training course.

(v) The women beneficiaries should be encouraged to consume the supplement food on the spot. Weight monitoring of the pregnant women and recording of birth weights should be made mandatory.

(vi) The Anganwadi Workers must make it a point to use the growth charts to educate the mothers. Further, mothers of severely malnourished children should be personally contacted by the health staff during their visits to the village.

(vii) The mothers should be well informed to raise the quality of post-natal care and also the MPW (Female) should be provided with the necessary tools so as to identify at risk mothers.

(viii) The Anganwadi Workers should use her own skills and aptitude to develop toys, games and charts using locally available material to enhance the quality of pre-school education.

(ix) The ICDS functionaries should initiate for the attitudinal change on the part of the community as well as bureaucracy to elicit community participation.

(x) Considering the honorary nature of work, educational background and work load of the

Anganwadi Workers, it is essential to limit the number of records and registers maintained by her. The following registers, if maintained properly can serve the purpose; *(a)* survey register *(b)* enrolment/ attendance! SN distribution registers can be grouped into one; *(c)* immunization records; *(d)* Growth charts including birth weights and *(e)* Food and drug stock register.

(xi) Looking at the administrative set-up it can be suggested that an additional body purely local in character which may be called local council should be set-up and linked with the administrative or bureaucratic organization in some way or the other. Secondly, in order to avoid the deficiencies in the working of the system, there must be a built-in arrangement for a regular monthly meeting of CD PO, PHC staff, Supervisors, MPWs and LHVs. On paper arrangements for such meetings do exist but rarely such meetings take place.

The study has highlighted some gaps in the functioning of Mahila MandalslWomen Groups and their role in strengthening the services of ICDS programme. In view of this, a few recommendations are given below:

(i) The objectives of the Mahila Mandals may be redesigned and following activities should also be included; *(a)* help children in getting admission in the school; *(b)* monitor the programmes related to women and children; *(c)* work for attitudinal changes among males; and *(d)* organise awareness camp etc.

(ii) Since a number of programmes of social and economic welfare were also being implemented by different departments and voluntary organisations, it will be pragmatic to ensure that their activities do not overlap. For this, suitable machinery for coordination

at the central and state will have to be evolved to avoid duplication.

(iii) Mostly the programmes are channelised through the block organisation. Hence, it is suggested that all department/agencies should carry out their work in relation to Mahila Mandals in rural areas.

(iv) A model constitution for Mahila Mandals is required for smooth functioning. It may be recast keeping in view the broad policy approach in respect of women and child development.

(v) The Extension Officer, who is an important functionary to look after the Mahila at the block level, should be fully responsible for the proper working of the Mandals. There is also the need to upgrade the professional skills of the existing extension staff so that they may involve rural women in the scheme.

(vi) For coordination of activities and better implementation of the scheme, the women member of the Gram Panchayat should also be included in the executive committee as a co-opted member.

(vii) In the ICDS blocks, a network of Mahila. Mandals should be set up to serve as a potent institution for mobilizing community participation. The functioning of district and village level coordination committee needs to be monitored to improve coordination.

(viii) In order to make the Mahila Mandals to act as change-agents, all efforts should be made to ensure participation of members from all sections of the village population irrespective of class, caste or religion.

(ix) The office-bearers of the Mahila Mandals should be given training in office procedures and accounting.

All the activities should be based on the felt-needs of women and children in an area and they should be related to what they are accustomed to. What is required is to improve their skills in such activities as may provide avenues for self-employment.

(x) Funds of Mahila Mandals should be raised through income generating activities, and contribution from villagers in the form of cash, labour and land for construction of their buildings. Cultural programmes and special drives may be organised during festivals and similar other occasions, to raise funds.

(xi) With a view to ensure the participation of socially and economically weaker sections, the Mahila Mandals should be oriented towards the needs of the deprived sections of the community and the activities, which are of interest to them.

(xii) Despite some limitations, it is evident that the Mandals have a great potential to play an important role in the ICDS scheme. What is needed is to lend them adequate support for the purpose. This calls for a pragmatic policy for revitalising them in such a way that they are able to enlist the cooperation of women from all sections of the society and also help them in improving their economic and social status.

(xiii) Efforts should be made towards construction of community house for carrying out the activities of Mahila Mandals so that women from the weaker sections do not suffer from social inhibitions.

10

National Commission for Women

The National Commission for Women is a product of the women's movement in the country. Parliamentarians and legislators gave the needed push to the passing of the National Commission for Women Act, 1990. The National Commission for Women (NCW) was constituted to perform various functions including investigation and examination of all matters relating to safeguards for women under the Constitution and other laws. The Commission has also to review from time to time, the existing provisions of the Constitution and laws affecting women and recommend amendments thereto so as to Suggest remedial legislative measures to meet the lacunae or shortcomings in such legislation. Through its various expert committees on laws and legislation, the Commission has examined and formulated measures to fill areas where there are no laws, such as domestic crimes and look into the adoption of abandored and destitute children, the common marriage bill, compulsory registration of marriages, etc. While looking into complaints on violence against women and also vidation of legal provisions and safeguards for women, the National Commission could take *suo motu* notice of matters relating to deprivation of women's rights, non-implementation of laws, in order to provide protection to women and also to achieve the objective of equality and development. Besides, it could take action where non-compliance of policy decisions, guidelines or instructions were aimed at mitigating hardship and ensuring welfare and providing relief to women.

Activities

The first and foremost case that of Poonam Balua, may be cited, where the victim was wrongly confined to jail after sunset and the police officer was persuading her to enter flesh trade to earn adequate riches. Almost a secret investigation made by NCW of this case resulted in dismissal of the police official concerned. It was a rare case, of a type wherein the police was fighting its own police vigilance department for having produced and corroborated the evidence given by the NCW. It is important to mention about this case as our first fight against victory gets gender justice. In spite of the fact that NCW has been especially set up as a statutory autonomous body, it is not to be equated with the role of crime against women's cell or an NGO or any other institution fighting individually and collectively for safeguarding women's rights. However, the NCW being the apex body on whom a lot of confidence has been reposed by the society and especially by the women at large, NCW took upon itself the onus of taking up certain exemplary cases which would have wider impact on maximum number of women in the country. Banwari Devi's gang-rape in Bateri village in Rajasthan has been a case in point. It is because of NCW's investigation and insistence and persuasion, that the Prime Minister came forward to offer an immediate relief to the victim and also through the CBI to thoroughly investigate the case and book the culprit. While one accused was arrested the other two are still absconding.

The NCW's intervention in this case catapulted focus on atrocities against rural women and Saathins who are state functionaries. This acted as a deterrent against violence on women—village functionaries like ICDS, the Saathins, gram, etc. Another case that needs mention is the timely intervention of NCW in a stripping case of Usha Dhiman, of Saharanpur who was a prey to the unruly elements and land mafia. Strangely, in the presence of police personnel, Usha Dhiman was stripped in public and was not lent a helping hand by anyone including the police. It was at the NCW's behest that an enquiry was conducted, transfers of concerned officials have been effected and due punishment was given. Similarly, in village Kutra, a tribal woman named Basanti Bara was elected as the President of the Panchayat and she has alleged that the State Minister for Tribals and Women Welfare of Orissa, who came to inaugurate the community centre, started molesting her in public. Her complaint reached NCW and the NCW, with its powers of a civil court, could summon the collector, the DSP and various officials, the victim and also the accused minister. These are some instances that could be quoted as NCW's successful fight against gender injustice. There are other instances and cases of grievances that we have received and attended to but the Commission cannot boast of solving all the cases. The Jayashankarpur (Orissa) village gang rape case by the police force was totally subdued by the local politicians, administration and the police. NCW's record has so far shown how party politics, caste or religious affiliations hinder the commitment to help the women who have been afflicted by various crimes. Apart from investigating various cases could investigate and summon witnesses and get the guilty punished through existing judicial delivery system, the NCW could organise a variety of conferences, workshops and seminars, where issues pertaining to gender bias are discussed and recommendations are forwarded to the concerned authorities for implementation. Though the Commission is short of adjudicatory powers, it has the power to persuade and advise the planning process of socio-economic development of women. Its contribution to the reforms in jails and especially in getting non-criminal lunatic convicts and under trials released is significant. Various jails are inspected and the NCW is organising sensitisation programmes for I.G. Prisons, and prison and police officials.

The Commission could also undertake promotional and educational research to find out ways of ensuring due representation of women in all spheres and identify factors responsible for impeding their advancement and growth such as, lack of access to housing and basic services, inadequate support services and technologies for reducing drudgery and occupational hazards, and in increasing their productivity. About 36-40 reports have been produced and various recommendations have already been sent to the concerned ministries/departments for implementation.

In its crusade against discrimination, violation of women's rights/human rights and the ever continuing gender injustice, the NCW has successfully gained recognition by the Supreme Court and various commissions who advised the Commission to prepare guidelines by which some respite and cheer could be brought to the unfortunate women victims. The Commission also funds, to some extent, litigation involving issues affecting a large body of women and makes periodical reports to the Government, both at the Centre and the State. The Central Government has referred a number of laws that needed amendment and there is constant interaction and consultations with the Ministry of Home Affairs, Ministry of Health, Department of Women and Child Development Ministry of Human Resource Development, Ministry of Welfare, etc.

The Commission has also successfully intervened against the Kerala Christian Bill denying Christian women's right to inheritance to property. Mary Roy's is a case in point. NCW has decided to intervene in the case filed in the Supreme Court by senior citizens of Karnataka against 33.33 per cent reservation of women in Panchayati Raj and local sabha governments. They proposed to challenge the 73rd and 74th Amendments to the Constitution on ground that the aforesaid

Amendments are contrary to the equality provision in the Constitution. (For extracts of 73rd and 74th Amendents of the Constitution refer Appendix II). We requested senior advocates of the Supreme Court in all these cases to represent the NCW including the case of Khartoonisa Begum's on the question of *Fatwa*. In spite of the fact that the Commission has been empowered to enter into all areas pertaining to women's issues and problems, the NCW feels that the remote village women still remain outside the precincts of justice.

Status of NCW

State Commissions for Women functioning in several States of India and this will be a part of Our networking. Now there are twelve Commission for women in the states of, Assam, Delhi, Karnataka, Kerala, Maharashtra, Orissa, Tamil Nadu, Tripura, West Bengal, Goa, Himachal Pradesh and Madhya Pradesh. These Commissions are very enthusiastic in seeking guidelines from the National Commission and also in feeding us with information on the status of women in their respective States. They are free to refer cases, which may be beyond their jurisdiction. Each State police system takes notice of this fact and tries to establish contacts with the State Commission so that this becomes a happy, alliance in search of justice for women.

Not a day passes, without the headlines in newspapers screaming, murder, mayhem or rape of women, even in the capital city of the country. This is not to say that there are no murders of men and children. The country is facing, as never before a torrent of crime, due to various socioeconomic reasons not to speak of infiltration of illegal, migrants, besides enemy State sponsored terrorism to strike at innocent victims, be they women and children or other citizens.

However, the worst-affected in this crime scenario are the women, as biologically they are vulnerable to sexual assault, rape, mass rape and gang rape, often committed by ruffians and the criminal factions to settle old scores with their rivals and enemies. Much of this kind of heinous crimes and atrocities have their roots in the drug mafia, foreign patronage and enemy country strategies to destabilise the civilian population, women and children and strike terror in their hearts. Planting of crude bombs, human bombs, exploiting women as suicide bombers have all now become a part of the criminal pattern.

This being briefly the crime pattern where do we go from here. Arresting of further crime and criminals creeping into society in the garb of respectable or even common citizens and devising various ways and strategies for prevention of crime must be made the fundamental base for grappling with this enormous problem, which is indeed a global phenomenon today.

Objectives of NCW

One of the chief objectives of the National Commission for Women is to ensure the safety and security of all women, as a prelude towards their progress and development. We must explore every possibility for prevention of crime and also bring to book the criminals who have perpetrated such crimes as rape, bride-burning and dowry deaths. But this is no easy task.

Statistics tell us that a woman is raped every hour, a dowry death occurs every one-and—a half hours and a woman is molested every hour somewhere or the other in the country. Also, every seven minutes an act of criminal offence against women is committed. There is an alarming increase and rise in crime from year to year, in dowry deaths and marital cruelty. This is indeed a grim situation.

Many factors linked to the growth of crime are, no doubt, beyond the control of police. As far back as in 1970, a United Nations Congress on Prevention of Crime identified some crimogenic factors, these are: urbanisation, industrialisation, population growth, outpacing the availability of housing, water supply, and other civic services, internal migration, not to speak of illegal migration, rapid technological changes in transport and communication techniques, which aid the international criminals to operate globally under cover of secrecy and thus cover their tracks.

A recent study of the working of the police reveals a considerable number among them are virtually untrained and not able or equipped to grapple or cope with critical situations, particularly due to mass recruitment of constables without fulfilling even the minimum requirements, often due to graft practices. In the process, many recruits with even a shady criminal past and record have managed to get inducted into the police force, both at the Centre and of course in the States, making a mockery of all procedures including routine police character certification. An ordinary citizen has to clear himself at so many levels before even a minor appointment either in the Government or even in the public or private sectors, but the guardians of law often skip these essential and vital formalities looming large over the civilians transcending and transgressing all laws.

In this context the Vohra Committee report of the former Home Secretary, acquires special significance. In this report, he was assisted by the heads of the Intelligence Bureau, Central Bureau of Investigation, and other experts but many of the recommendations, now over two years old are yet to be implemented and are collecting dust. These have not even been debated, mainly because the report has underscored the evils and repercussions of the continual and near perpetual criminal nexus of the unscrupulous; politicians with the underworld dons and mafia. Also, over the years the criminals themselves get elected to local bodies and finally attain political stature, with immense evil and destructive powers to use every kind of luxury as perceived by them and mainly young women become pawns in their game.

The Vested Interests

The criminal-political nexus has acquired and sustained such incredible power that they are able to subvert the country's law and order scenario, jeopardising the daily lives of the common citizens, worst-affected being women and children. Solutions to this grim scenario of crime and therefore crime prevention are aplenty. But it is only through pressure groups and public opinion that the Government may be expected to act. Justice V.R. Krishna Iyer said: "A tireless and zealous worker in this field has very often underscored the importance of a separate sophisticated force, with special skills, drills, techniques, technology and aloof from the f03silising near feudal setup. A special ethos, ethic and professionalism are absolutely essential to meet the challenge of criminal cunning, the menace of macabre intricacies and the subtle machinations of criminals and this force must of course not resort to vulgarity, violence or any other vice."

The apathy of police stations to accept FIRs brought specially by women, the women under trials languishing in jails because of police delays in filing reports in the courts, are serious matters to be attended to. There has to be an ongoing sensitisation and training programme for the lower levels of police personnel. This is an urgent need since the police personnel have very often been ignoring the special legislation on dowry, sati, etc. A proper understanding by the lower police force that women's rights are humar, rights is very essential and important.

We are not for once under rating the various disabilities faced by the police as a system. The inadequacy of staff, lack of modern gadgetry, the various laws and procedures inhibiting their functioning are common knowledge.

Moreover the police, which cannot be totally independent of the executive must devise ways and means for a minimum of operational independence particulars in the discharge of statutory duties and responsibilities. The National Police Commission has suggested that this can be ensured by regulating the transfers of officials and giving them a fixed tenure and also fixing specific duties/responsibilities in a time-bound frame. A suggestion was also made to setup statutory commissions. State-wise in order to contain sometimes erratic transfer exercises by the executive, which disrupt the smooth coordinated functioning of the police force.

A band of women constables must be recruited in each district, each town and city, preferably with proximity to the rural areas, to enable them to ensure the security and safety of the women and child population and to check crime and book the criminals. We are proud of women police officers like Kiran Bedi, and others, who while doing a yeoman service in the preservation and sustenance of a smooth and coordinated law and order system, continue to direct their attention to some of the criminal patterns, crucial and peculiar to the women population and provide safety guidelines for custodialrape and torture, miscarriage of justice and in proven cases of guilt, find ways and means of reformation as also through deterrent policies for the rest of the people.

The police is also in a dilemma, for, if they act effectively, they are charged with excesses. If they do not, they are accused of inaction. Now we have to exchange views and ideas and sort out the chaotic situation, arising out of a degenerating society, which has lost its moral fibre to a great extent and which in turn has generated an uncontrollable growth of crime and violence. At the risk of repetition, one must stress that it is the common woman who finds it impossible to stir out after dusk, alone, even during an emergency, not to speak of daylight molestations, eve-teasing, rape, robberies and murders, kidnapping, abduction and sometimes bride-burning.

New: The Ray of Hope for Women

It is an accepted fact that, even on the threshold of the 21st century, there is no section of our society Chore oppressed, more exploited and more neglected than women. In every segment, class or community, women suffer all the disabilities inflicted on that group and in addition, suffer the consequences of gender discrimination too. Yet, their contribution in economic life, social well-being, cultural continuity and ethical standards is far greater than their share of the population.

A national daily of Delhi commented on 29th January, 1995 under the caption 'Cries of Oppression' that, "while we progress technologically, earning ourselves a reputation for a world of satellites, missiles and fifth generation computers, we have also acquired the distinction of recording one rape in every 42 minutes, besides increased cases of crimes against women, including molestation, stripping, eve-teasing, kidnapping, dowry deaths, female foeticide, even sati, and the lakhs of women who are abused and battered by their husbands in the privacy of their own homes. The National Commission for Women (NCW) is now in the process of hearing tales of atrocities committed on hapless women across the country, but the women who appeared before the NCW's bench of jurors and social: workers cannot be assured of justice as the Commission does not have 'teeth or nails', it can only make recommendations. Most of the cases heard are about dowry deaths, sexual harassment at the workplace, rape, desertion and being refused alimony after divorce. "My only ray of hope is the NCW, said a mother, whose daughter was burnt to death for not giving enough dowry." Such is the confidence, such are the expectations and such are the demands that the women of the country have of the Commission.

On the completion of its tenure of five years, an evaluation of the national forum might be appropriate. A legitimate question that might arise in one's mind would be how well did the NCW fare in its search and endeavour for striving to secure equality, justice and fair treatment in all that matters in the life of women for their honourable existence without oppression, denial of opportunities and deprivation of rights.

Origin

It may be recalled that the NCW was constituted on 31st January, 1992 under the National Commission for Women Act, 1990. NCW Act, 1990 is a statute having the potential to catalyse all the arms of the State under parliamentary democracy, *i.e.* the legislature, the executive and the judiciary, though much more powers could make the Commission an effective instrument to be of substantive assistance to the aggrieved women. When we sit in judgement to evaluate the work done during its five years existence, we would perhaps be perplexed by the spontaneous and overwhelming response its work has aroused in the shape of hopes and expectations as also that of dissatisfaction in some cases.

Structure, Objectives and Functions

To mention briefly the structure, objectives and functions of the Commission, it is composed of a permanent national forum of seven full time members consisting of a Chairperson, five members and a member-secretary. The Commission's functions cover every aspect of women's concerns and issues. They range from protective laws and constitutional provisions to empowerment. Specifically, these functions are to: *(a)* take up the cases of violation of the provisions of the Constitution and of other laws relating to women, *(b)* look into complaints and fake *suo moto* notice of matters relating to: deprivation of women's rights, non-implementation of laws enacted to provide protection to women and also to achieve the objective of equality and development, non-compliance of policy decisions, guidelines or instructions aimed at mitigating hardships and ensuring welfare and providing relief to women and take up the issues arising out of such matter with appropriate authorities.

In addition, the Commission could *(a)* commission special investigations of specific problems related to discrimination and atrocities against women; *(b)* undertake promotional research to suggest ways of ensuring due representation of women in all spheres; *(c)* evaluate the progress of the development of women under the Union and in all States; *(d)* inspect jails, remand homes, and other institutions and places of custody where women are lodged voluntarily or involuntarily.

While investigating complaints NCW has the powers of a civil court in trying a suit; it can summon and enforce the attendance of any person, and examine that person under oath, as well as require the production of relevant documents, etc.

While discussing on the theme, one cannot resist quoting Justice V.R. Krishna lyer. In one of his works he stated that:

Women's welfare is legislated galore but remain paper tigers since men are to implement it. That compounds the crime, since even policemen are if reports are correct, among criminals who endanger women. Even the laws are so lacunose that the judiciary, if objectively judged, will be found guilty... Women must be awakened as has happened in the anti-attack campaign of Andhra Pradesh women. Social awareness is the beginning of radical change. A massive campaign involving the vast masses of illiterate women, is necessitous all over India.

Taking full cognizance of Justice Krishna Iyer's observations and also after evaluating the work done during the three year tenure of earlier Commission, and identified some thrust areas to bring about perceptible results in dealing with women's concerns. These were:

— Speedy Justice for Women (through Parivarik Milhila Lok Adalats)

- Legal Awareness Programme for Women Colleges
- Custodial Justice
- Steps Towards Rehabilitation of
- Women & Children in Prostitution
- Widows
- Blind Women
- Destitutes and
- Anti-Arrack Campaign.

Till the end of July' 97, NCW, through the good offices of District Legal Aid Society, the Judiciary and NGOs have held about 100 Parivarik Mahila Lok Adalats. By no means is this a mean achievement in that it has handled about 5700 cases. In the field of legal awareness campaign, we have sponsored through NGOs, 35 training camps/workshops coupled with Panchayati Raj training for women. Further, 180 women's colleges were covered to give legal training to 200 teachers and 5000 girl students and others. This again is an innovative step, the results of which would be sustainable and widespread.

Another important area is that of legal literacy for visually handicapped women. With the cooperation of the Sunanda Bhandare Foundation, 60 blind women were given training during 1997.

According to a report on prohibition and development of women to ensure that anti-arrack-movement is taken to its logical conclusion in achieving total prohibition.

We can cite innumerable cases and specific areas handled by NCW recently. These cover the critical concerns, such as:

(i) Outraging modesty of women, also involving persons in high eminence.

(*ii*) Atrocities on women, *e.g.* Uttarakhand

(*iii*) Dowry harassment, dowry death

(*iv*) Harassment at workplace

(*v*) Gender based denial of opportunities

NCW's effort in mobilising support for 81st Constitutional Amendment Bill providing for 33-1/3 per cent reservation in Lok Sabha and State legislatures are too well known needing no elaboration.

Processing of complaints, commissioning witnesses where necessary constituted an important function. The· impetus for entertaining a few representative individual complaints came from tales of woes of umpteen harassed women explained in various complaints both written and oral that the Commission were receiving both in office and during tours of Chairperson, Members and the Member Secretary. The harassed women were running from pillar to post to seek justice. During its tenure, it received a total of about 800 complaints relating broadly to dowry, murder and dowry related atrocities, disputes over matrimonial properties, rape and molestation, harassment at workplaces, desertions and other atrocities. In most of the cases, it has been possible for the Commission to take up the issues with the concerned authorities and persuade them to set right the wrongs done.

Realising the intensity, gravity and volume of the work in the complaint cell of NCW, we have added counselling and prelitigation services round the clock to offer prompt and effective assistance to the aggrieved women.

Assessing NCW's performance, at the end of its three years' term, a Calcutta (Now Kolkata) English daily in an issue of February 2, 1995 commented: "Should one just dismiss it as a weak offspring of the government and an appendage that has disillusioned those who fought for its creation? Or should one give it credit for its first few tottering steps towards getting women a better deal from the government and the society at large? Or perhaps the NCW qualifies for both brickbats and bouquets, if one takes into account its vast but powerful mandate and its list of achievements."

We are confident that when one would make an assessment at the end of NCW's six-year term in 1998, the number of bouquets would heavily outnumber the brickbats. It must be admitted that the issues are so large that NCW would need vastly improved powers, facilities and cooperation from all concerned to make the life of Indian women better than today.

Status of State Commissions

We had been pursuing with various States the question of setting up of Women's Commission and had expected several more State Commissions to have been formed by this time, but most of the States have not found it feasible so far in spite of assurances. We hope that 1996 will witness the constitution of Women's Commission at least in all major States like Uttar Pradesh, Madhya Pradesh, Bihar, Rajasthan, Karnataka, Haryana, Andhra Pradesh and others.

The three-year term of the first National Commission for Women came to an end on 31st January, 1995 except for one member who had not completed three years. Weeks, and then months, passed by without the vacancies being filled with the result that only one member and the member secretary carried on the Commission work until July, 1995 when the Chairperson and four other members were nominated. The intervening six months were utilised to complete the ongoing projects and other pending work, drawing up future plans, convening a conference of the State Commissions, organising two or three seminars/ workshops, taking stock of the work done in the preceding years and attending to some other issues Like drafting our part for the Country Paper for Beijing Conference. Ms Padma Seth joined us as Member in

January, 1996. Last March, two members resigned. Thus, the Commission is now short of two members. A new member secretary, Dr Nisha Sahai Achuttan, joined us only a couple of weeks back.

On assuming charge, the Commission work at a breakneck speed so as to make up for the loss of six months. The achievements of the Commission during this one year period are many and we are satisfied. In order to bring a quick settlement of women's cases pending in civil courts for long periods, the Commission organised Parivarik Mahila Adalats in various States, taking assistance of the State's Legal Boards and the judiciary, and actively associating the local NGOs in organising the Adalats. So far, settlement in more than one thousand cases have been reached, with Gujarat taking a lead. The State Commission to give a fillip to the Mahila Lok Adalats in their States, NGO's have taken up seriously with the State Governments, the question of release of undertrial women prisoners who have been languishing in jails for unnecessarily prolonged periods Similarly, the question of premature release of women life convicts under Article 161 of the Constitution and of term convicts under section 432 of Cr. P.C. is also being pursued. We understand that Andhra Pradesh Government recently issued orders for release all undertrial women who had been in jail for more than a year. I hope you will vigorously pursue the issue of the release of women prisoners in your States with the respective authorities.

The Commission has undertaken a large-scale programme for creating legal awareness among women. For this purpose, we have tied up with the National Law School, Bangalore where selected lady teachers of women's colleges from all over the country are trained in legal matters pertaining to women and they in turn hold legal awareness classes for girl students of their colleges. Another action plan of the Commission has been to give impetus to the anti-arrack movement in the country. Liquor, as we all know, is a major cause of ruin of many poor and middle class homes. Women's groups in several States have started anti-arrack movements, with marked success at a number of places. The Commission aims to bring into a network the various women's groups all over the country engaged in anti-arrack struggle so as to create a strong lobby against the evils of liquor. A workshop to strengthening the movement has been mooted.

The Commission has also been making efforts towards rescue and rehabilitation of children from brothels and of women forced into mental asylums.

The Commission took up cases of injustice done to widows and has initiated, with the help of NGOs, rehabilitation programmes in Mathura and Vrindawan.

With regard to political empowerment, adequate representation of women in Parliament and State Legislatures has been pursued by the Commission and the results are now before you.

In a vast country like ours, with a variety of customs and social values, different languages and different levels of education and economic development, the problems facing women differ from region to region. Many of them are area specific, some others specific to communities and groups. A good number of these problems fall within the domain of respective States and can best be handled by the State Commissions. The National Commission for Women has to look into the issues of wider common interests. It is, therefore, essential that every State should have a Women's Commission.

It is of utmost importance that a close liaison is maintained between the National and State Women's Commissions and a good measure of coordination and collaboration in their activities attained so that the recommendations on the issues are not divergent or conflicting. For instance, there are many women-specific Central laws and also numerous provisions in IPC. They are all under constant review and examination by the National Commission. In a number of cases, State Commissions have also gone into these issues and recommended amendments according to their own perceptions. In such a situation, the recommendations of various Commissions on the same issue may turn out to be different from each other. We must speak with a united voice, if we are to be effective. The best course would therefore, be that in legislative matters having national purport, the views of the State Commissions are forwarded to the National Commission for framing recommendations. Networking is thus of great value in avoiding duplication of effort and also for achieving general consensus on crucial Issues.

No development process can bear fruit without enlisting the cooperation and support of NGOs, the vital link in connecting people with the administration. It was an excellent idea mooted in the last meeting that the State Commission prepare a directory of NGOs working for women in their States along with brief description of the field of their expertise as also a list of experts in various areas related to women.

Another idea of great value broached last time was to prepare a statewise database on women. Database is the most important input in preparing strategies or programmes for women's welfare and development the State Commissions have made good progress in this sphere as well.

The Scope and Reach of New

NCW has been a ray of hope and inspiration to our women and NCWA it is significant that the National Commission for Women Act, a product of sustained and committed women's movement in our country, was enacted during the Janata Dal government headed by Shri V.P. Singh. We all know that your enlightened leadership is committed to uphold social justice and we women can except more than a fair deal in matters of deprivation, injustice and inequality. The evidence is not far to seek. The announcement by your government of one-third reservation for women in state legislatures and parliament augurs well and speaks volumes regarding your concern for empowerment of women.

While we welcome our government's commitments we also would urge that in all structures of governance—economic, social and political—expert groups and policy making positions should include women.

NCW was setup specifically to be an autonomous statutory body, an independent commission, which would have the "independence" to interact with the government the state as well as society accountable for women's condition. It was even thought at one time to model it on the concept of the Lok Ayukt so that it would be particularly directed to redress discrimination against women, the inequality between men and women across all barriers.

In order for it to perform this role of acting as a guardian of women's rights, to prevent as well as to make amends for injustice done to women, by definition it had to be genuinely independent both in its constitutional construction as well as in its operational instruments and process. The NCW Act is a welcome legislation. It would be more effective if it is vested with some more investigating, prosecuting and implementing powers within the broad framework of our constitutional scheme of judiciary and executive and parliamentary system of democracy.

With your blessings, we would like to review the constitution and procedures of NCW and the administrative linkage of the commission with the ministry and reformulate the act and the procedures of the commission such that it can truly be a monitoring body, provide annual reports to the government, scruntinise and advise on recommendations on policy made by the government on behalf of all those groups in India who have, with such courage and wisdom, safeguarded and moved forward women's rights in India.

We would like it to be a bridge between what is called the civic society, the non-governmental sector and women's voluntary organizations, who are deeply in touch with the daily lives of the women, their problems, and their abilities and viewpoints. The commission was designed to be a bridge between this lively broad-based constituency of women's organisations and the government.

This particular moment in the Indian political evolution is of interest and significance to the Indian women's participation in national development. A coalition government, which brings together regional parties and national parties provides for women the kind of opportunity that they have always sought. Women, as you know, tend to come together as women' which is more important to them than their identities as people belonging to a political party or a religion or a caste. There is a bonding amongst women, which provides a natural platform of solidarity. With the formation of the coalition government, women see two great opportunities-first, they can come together as 'women' and know that the government being a coalition provides a unified platform for them. Secondly, a coalition government is seeking a common minimum programme, a consensus and a direction. Women are a natural coalition across class, caste and political parties and can provide this mechanism for a coalition government to implement its policies.

To enable us to perform this role of expressing the woman citizen's voice and holding the State society accountable, we are developing a monitoring framework, some new indices of measurement which would indicate effective utilisation of programme as well as its impact on reduction of poverty and inequality. The Commission and the State level Commissions with the help of women's movement namely the voluntary organisations would like to build up the capability to be able to ensure that the delivery arrangements for this programme are efficient and they reach those for whom they are meant We would also like to develop mechanisms of accountability where we can monitor the delivery, draw attention of the public and the elected bodies to what is right and what is 'wrong and make sure that this objective gets fulfilled with the best use of the resources.

To enable us to perform this function, it would be very important for your government to invest in the women's movement funds and political support-funds and independence to the National Commission and the State Commissions.

We have now twelve State Commissions for Women. Now we hope to get established Commissions for Women in each of the remaining States. The State Commissions for Women must be accorded a status commensurate with functions, decorum, protocol and expectations that the government and the people have of NCW, still it is common knowledge that when dealing with men and matters the status counts a lot and its absence has many a time created embarrassment and lack of results.

The poverty and destitution, especially that faces by women, girls and female infants. Poor women are successful in providing and managing financial services for themselves through innovative structures like chit fund, self-help group cooperatives, etc. These efforts need to be taken note of in designing financial committees at all levels and their experience should be included in the formulation of policy.

However, within this category there are some women such as widows, prostitutes and women prisoners. We have in the last one year visited prisons, met widows, gone to red-light areas and with a great deal of intimate interaction have come up with specific ways in which we could relieve these women from what can be called the atrocities committed against them. It is the women's organisations, the Commissions on women in partnership with the government that are to redress and respond to these atrocities.

However, there are some key points on which we need to have your directions. A whole package of needs is required for those who are in prostitution ranging from children, to their health that requires the attention of the government. Amongst many of the things the prostitutes have asked for is that raids should not be made in red-light areas, and you can understand it because these raids are usually made to further worsen the situation.

Another deep concern of women is the tremendous violence, which they experience when the men in their families are drunk. The anti-arrack movement, which is primarily associated with Andhra Pradesh, is not only in Andhra Pradesh. It has spread like wild fire in all the States in India. The National Commission for Women called a meeting of women engaged in anti-arrack struggles and found that it was flooded with requests to attend from groups starting from Uttarakhand going all the way to Kanyakumari. On the West, from Goa, Maharashtra to Orissa in the East, all wanted to belong to what they call a "Mukti Manch", they want freedom for their village from the violence of alcohol. They asked for 'Gram Swaraj, the word that Gandhiji used. They wanted the gram to have Swaraj from arrack Freedom from liquor is the slogan they coined. Women have led the battle against bottle. In Andhra Pradesh, neo-literate women used broomsticks and chilli powder to force the closure or liquor shops. The stories they told were gruesome; husbands rapine daughters, because they could not distinguish them from their wives. And one woman said only when prohibition came in Andhra Pradesh were we able to sleep soundly. Earlier in 1992, women activists in Haryana torched a liquor shop sparking off a State wide movement. Almost similar tactics, as in Haryana were adopted by women in Kochi, Kerala. Today, there is a ban on sale of arrack in Kerala.

On the reverse side the economic argument that there is a loss in excise is not true. In Andhra Pradesh, according to the officials, household incomes of poor households has gone up by Rs. 500 as a result of non-consumption of alcohol. In turn these household are now buying rice, vegetables, cloth and generate a demand in the market, which adds to the economies buoyancy. They have also, for example, saved seven crores in one district as savings from this additional income. It is well-known that what is lost in excise revenue is more than made up in sales tax revenue by the amount of goods that are purchased with the money saved form liquor. What is less recorded but is equally important is the fact that the health of men, women and children improves because of the food that is available with the increased income. And this sure saves money on health services. There will also be money for them to be spent on children's education and so forth. Therefore, there is an additional increase in revenue which is invisible but which saves money for the exchequer.

We know of your great concern for rural areas of India and for the poor. From the women's point of view it is removal of arrack, namely implementation of prohibition in a more widespread way that is even more important than providing employment. Because the money saved from liquor is income for women and children. We eagerly look forward to hearing your response to our ideas and hopes.

One of the most important issues of against women is the wages that women receive notwithstanding Equal Remuneration Act. Women's wages are always lower than men very unjustly because they work hard if not harder than men, whether it is on roads, farms, fields, etc. Thus, we would like to safeguard and implement the Equal Remuneration Act and also make sure that the valuation of women's work is reflected in their wages.

The district taluka and village are the most important theatres for action and redressal for women. Women like those engaged in anti-arrack or chipko have found the need for district committee with some legal and statutory powers to direct the administration. We, at the Commission would like to be deeply involved in all the discussions and plans for development.

Our government's most important unifying, platforms is secularism. Women, more than any other category of people have a bonding and identity which goes beyond caste, religion and class. We would like to offer the large and widespread network of women's organisations as those who will make the most earnest efforts to build communal harmony. We would like to have consultations with women from different religious groups and build with them a platform of a common minimum programme.

HUMAN RIGHTS OF WOMEN

- Human rights and fundamental freedoms are the birthright of all human beings; their protection and promotion is the first responsibility of Governments.

- The World Conference on Human Rights reaffirmed the solemn commitment of all States to fulfill their obligation to promote universal respect for, and observance and protection of, all human rights and fundamental freedoms for all, in accordance with the Charter of the United Nations other instruments relating to human rights, and international law. The universal nature of these rights and freedoms is beyond question.

- The promotion and protection of all human rights and fundamental freedoms must be considered as a priority objective of the United Nations, in accordance with its purposes and principles, in particular with the purpose of international cooperation. In the framework of these purposes and principles, the promotion and protection of all human rights is a legitimate concern of the international community. The international community must treat human rights globally, in a fair and equal manner, on the same footing, and with the same emphasis. The Platform for Action reaffirms the importance of ensuring the universality, objectivity and non-selectivity of the consideration of human rights issues.

• The Platform for Action reaffirms that all human rights-civil, cultural, economic, political and social, including the right to development—are universal, indivisible, interdependent and interrelated, as expressed in the Vienna Declaration and Programme of Action adopted by the World Conference on Human Rights. The Conference reaffirmed that the human rights of women and the girl child are an inalienable, integral and indivisible part of universal human rights. The full and equal enjoyment of all human rights and fundamental freedoms by women and girls is a priority for Governments and the United Nations and is essential for the advancement of women.

• Equal rights of men and women are explicitly mentioned in the Preamble to the Charter of the United Nations. All the major international human rights instruments include sex as one of the grounds upon which States may not discriminate.

• Governments must not only refrain from violating the human rights of all women, but must work actively to promote and protect these rights. Recognition of the importance of the human rights of women of reflected m the fact that three quarters of the States Members of the United Nations have become parties to the Convention on the Elimination of All Forms of Discrimination against Women.

• The World Conference on Human Rights reaffirmed clearly that the human rights of women throughout the life cycle are an inalienable, integral and indivisible part of universal human rights. The International Conference on Population and Development reaffirmed women's reproductive rights and the right to development. Both the Declaration of the Rights of the Child [31] and the Convention on the Rights of the Child [11] guarantee children's rights and uphold the principle of nondiscrimination on the grounds of gender.

• The gap between the existence of rights and their effective enjoyment derives from a lack of commitment by Governments to promoting and protecting those rights and the failure of Governments to inform women and men alike about them. The lack of appropriate recourse mechanisms at the national and international levels, and inadequate resources at both levels, compound the problem. In most countries, steps have been taken to reflect the rights guaranteed by the Convention on the Elimination of All Forms of Discrimination against Women in national law. A number of countries have established mechanisms to strengthen women's ability to exercise their rights.

• In order to protect the human rights of women it is necessary to avoid, as far as possible, resorting to reservations and to ensure that no reservation is incompatible with the object and purpose of the Convention or is otherwise incompatible with international treaty law. Unless the human rights of women, as defined by international human rights instruments, are fully recognized and effectively protected, applied, implemented and enforced in national law as well as in national practice in family civil, penal, labour and commercial codes and administrative rules and regulations, they will exist in name only.

• In those countries that have not yet become parties to the Convention on the Elimination of All Forms of Discrimination against Women and other international human rights instruments, or where reservations that are incompatible with the object or purpose of the Convention have been entered, or where national laws have not yet been revised to implement international norms and standards, women's de jure equality is not yet secured. Women's full enjoyment of equal rights is undermined by the discrepancies between some national legislation and international law and international instruments on human rights. Overly complex administrative procedures, lack of awareness within the judicial process and inadequate monitoring of the violation of the human rights of all women, coupled with the under-representation of women in justice systems, insufficient information on existing rights and persistent attitudes and practices perpetuate women's de facto inequality. De facto inequality is also perpetuated by the lack of enforcement of inter alia farmly civil, penal, labour and commercial laws or codes or administrative rules and regulations intended to ensure women's full enjoyment of human rights and fundamental freedoms.

- Every person should be entitled to participate in, contribute to and enjoy cultural, economic, political and social development. In many cases women and girls suffer discrimination in the allocation of economic and social resources. This directly violates their economic, social and cultural rights.

- The human rights of all women and the girl child must form an integral part of United Nations human rights activities. Intensified efforts are needed to integrate the equal status and the human rights of all women and girls into the mainstream of United Nations system-wide activities and to address these issues regularly and systematically throughout relevant bodies and mechanisms. This requires,' *inter alia,* improved cooperation and coordination between the Commission on the Status of Women, the United Nations High Commissioner for Human Rights, the Commission on Human Rights, including its special and thematic rapporteurs, independent experts, working groups and its Sub-commission on Prevention of Discrimination and Protection of Minorities, the Commission on Sustainable Development, the Commission for Social Development, the Commission on Crime Prevention and Criminal Justice, and the Committee on the Elimination of Discrimination against Women and other human rights treaty bodies, and all relevant entities of the United Nations system, including the specialized agencies. Cooperation is also needed to strengthen, rationalize and streamline the United Nations human rights system and to promote its effectiveness and efficiency, taking into account the need to avoid unnecessary duplication and overlapping of mandates and tasks.

• If the goal of full realization of human rights for all is to be achieved, international human rights instruments must be applied in such a way as to take more clearly into consideration the systematic and systemic nature of discrimination against women that gender analysis has clearly indicated.

• Bearing in mind the Programme of Action of the International Conference on Population and Development [14] and the Vienna Declaration and Programme of Action [2] adopted by the World Conference on Human Rights, the Fourth World Conference on Women reaffirms that reproductive rights rest on the recognition of the basic right of all couples and individuals to decide freely and responsibly the number, spacing and timing of their children and to have the information and means to do so, and the right to attain the highest standard of sexual and reproductive health. It also includes their right to make decisions concerning reproduction free of discrimination coercion and violence, as expressed in human right documents.

• Violence against women both violates and impairs or nullifies the enjoyment by women of human rights and fundamental freedoms. Taking into account the Declaration on the Elimination of Violence against Women and the work of Special Rapporteurs, gender-based violence such as battering and other domestic violence, sexual abuse, sexual slavery and exploitation, and international trafficking In women and children, forced prostitution and sexual harassment, as well as violence against women, resulting from cultural prejudice, racism and racial discrimination xenophobia, pornography, ethnic cleansing, armed conflict' foreign occupation, religious and anti-religious extremist and terrorism are incompatible with the dignity and the worth of the human person and must be combated and eliminated. Any harmful aspect of certain traditional customary or modern practices that violates the rights or women should be prohibited and eliminated. Governments' should take urgent action to combat and eliminate all forms of violence against women in private and public life, whether perpetrated or tolerated by the State or private persons.

- Many women face additional barriers to the enjoyment of their human rights because of such factors as their race, language, ethnicity, culture, religion, disability or socio-economic class or because they are indigenous people, migrants, including women migrant workers, displaced women or refugees. They may also be disadvantaged and marginalized by a general lack of knowledge and recognition of their human rights as well as by the obstacles they meet in gaining access to information and recourse mechanisms in cases of violation of their rights.

- The factors that cause the flight of refugee women, other displaced women in need of international protection and internally displaced women may be different from those affecting men. These women continue to be vulnerable to abuses of their human rights during and after their flight.

- While women are increasingly using the legal system to exercise their rights, in many countries lack of awareness of the existence of these rights is an obstacle that prevents women from fully enjoying their human rights and attaining equality. Experience in many countries has shown that women can be empowered and motivated to assert their rights, regardless of their level of education or socio-economic status. Legal literacy programmes and media strategies have been effective in helping women to understand the link between their rights and other aspects of their lives and in demonstrating that cost-effective initiatives can be undertaken to link women obtain those rights. Provision of human rights education is essential for promoting an understanding of the human rights of women, including knowledge of recourse mechanisms to redress violations of their rights. It is necessary for all individuals, especially women in vulnerable circumstances, to have full knowledge of their rights and access to legal recourse against violations of their rights.

• Women engaged in the defence of human rights must be protected. Governments have a duty to guarantee the full enjoyment of all rights set out in the Universal Declaration of Human Rights, the International Covenant on Civil and Political Rights and the International Covenant on Economic, Social and Cultural Rights by women working peacefully in a personal or organisational capacity for the promotion and protection of human rights. Nongovernmental organisations, women's organisations and feminist groups have played a catalytic role in the promotion of the human rights of women through grass-roots activities, networking and advocacy and need encouragement, support and access to information from Governments in order to carry out these activities.

• In addressing the enjoyment of human rights, Governments and other actors should promote art active and visible policy of mainstreaming a gender perspective in all policies and programmes so that, before decisions are taken, an analysis is made of the effects on women and men, respectively.

Strategic Objective

Promote and protect the human rights of women, through the full implementation of all human rights instruments, especially the Convention on the Elimination of All Forms of Discrimination against Women

Actions to be taken

- By Governments:

(*a*) Work actively towards ratification of or accession to and implement international and regional human rights treaties;

(*b*) Ratify and accede to and ensure implementation of the Convention on the Elimination of All Forms of Discrimination against Women so that universal ratification of the Convention can be achieved by the year 2000;

(*c*) Limit the extent of any reservations to the Convention on the Elimination of All Forms of Discrimination against Women; formulate any such reservations as precisely and as narrowly as possible; ensure that no reservations are incompatible with the object and purpose of the Convention or otherwise incompatible with international treaty law and regularly review them with a view to withdrawing them and withdraw reservations that are contrary to the object and purpose of the Convention on the Elimination of All Forms of Discrimination against Women or which are otherwise incompatible with international treaty law;

(*d*) Create or strengthen independent national institutions for the protection and promotlon of these rights, including the human rights of women, as recommended by the World Conference on Human Rights;

(*e*) Consider drawing up national action plans identifying steps to improve the promotion and protection of human rights, including the human rights of women, as recommended by the World Conference on Human Rights;

(f) Develop a comprehensive human rights education programme to raise awareness among women of their human rights and raise awareness among others of the human rights of women;

(g) If they are States parties, implement the Convention by reviewing all national laws, policies, practices and procedures to ensure that they meet the obligations set out in the Convention; all States should undertake a review of all national laws, policies, practices and procedures to ensure that they meet international human rights obligations in this matter;

(h) Report on schedule to the Committee on the Elimination of Discrimination against Women regarding the implementation of the Convention, following fully the guidelines established by the Committee and involving non-governmental organisations, where appropriate, or taking into account their contributions in the preparation of the report;

(i) Include gender aspects in reporting under all other human rights conventions and instruments, including ILO conventions, to ensure analysis and review of the human rights of women;

(j) Enable the Committee on the Elimination of Discrimination against Women fully to discharge its mandate by allowing for adequate meeting time through broad ratification of the revision adopted by the States parties to the Convention on the Elimination of All Forms of Discrimination against Women on 22 May 1995 relative to article 20, paragraph 1, [32] and by promoting efficient working methods;

(*k*) Address the acute problems of children, inter alia, by supporting efforts in the context of the United Nations system aimed at adopting efficient international measures for the prevention and eradication of female infanticide, harmful child labour, the sale of children and their organs, child prostitution, child pornography and other forms of sexual abuse and consider contributing to the drafting of an optional protocol to the Convention on the Rights of the Child;

(*l*) Support the process initiated by the Commission on the Status of Women with a view to elaborating a draft optional protocol to the Convention on the Elimination of All Forms of Discrimination against. Women that could enter into force as soon as possible on a right of petition procedure, taking into consideration the Secretary-General's report on the optional protocol, including those views related to its feasibility;

(*m*) Take urgent measures to achieve universal ratification of or accession to the Convention on the Rights of the Child before the end of 1995 and full implementation of the Convention in order to ensure equal rights for girls and boys; those that have not already done so are urged to become parties in order to realize universal implementation of the Convention on the Rights of the Child by the year 2000;

(*n*) Strengthen the implementation of all relevant human rights instruments in order to combat and eliminate, including through international cooperation, organized and other forms of trafficking in women and children including trafficking for the purposes of sexual exploitation, pornography, prostitution and sex tourism, and provide legal and social services to the victims; this should include provisions for international cooperation to prosecute and punish those responsible for organized exploitation of women and children;

(o) Taking into account the need to ensure full respect for the human rights of indigenous women, consider a declaration on the rights of indigenous people for adoption by the General Assembly within the International Decade of the World's Indigenous People and encourage the participation of indigenous women in the working group elaborating the draft declaration, in accordance with the provisions for the participation of organizations of indigenous people.

• By relevant organs, bodies and agencies of the United Nations system, all human rights bodies of the United Nations system, as well as the United Nations High Commissioner for Human Rights and the United Nations High Commissioner for Refugees, while promoting greater efficiency and effectiveness through better coordination of the various bodies, mechanisms and procedures, taking into account the need to avoid unnecessary duplication and overlapping of their mandates and tasks:

(a) Give full, equal and sustained attention to the human rights of women in the exercise of their respective mandates to promote universal respect for and protection of all human rights—civil, cultural, economic, political and social rights, including the right to development;

(b) Ensure the implementation of the recommendations of the World Conference on Human Rights for the full integration and mainstreaming of the human rights of women;

(*c*) Develop a comprehensive policy programme for mainstreaming the human rights of women throughout the United Nations system, including activities with regard to advisory services, technical assistance, reporting methodology, gender-impact assessments, coordination, public information and human rights education, and play an active role in the implementation of the programme;

(*d*) Include information on gender-based human rights violations in their activities and integrate the findings into all of their programmes and activities;

(*e*) Ensure the integration and full participation of women as both agents and beneficiaries in the development process and reiterate the, objectives established for global action for women towards sustainable and equitable development set forth in the Rio Declaration on Environment and Development; [18]

(*f*) Ensure that there is collaboration and coordination of the work of all human rights bodies and mechanisms to ensure that the human rights of women are respected;

(*g*) Strengthen cooperation and coordination between the Commission on the Status of Women, the Commission on Human Rights, the Commission for Social Development, the Commission on Sustainable Development, the Commission on Crime Prevention and Criminal Justice, the United Nations human rights treaty monitoring bodies, including the Committee on the Elimination of Discrimination against Women, and the United Nations Development Fund for Women, the International Research and Training Institute for the Advancement of Women, the United Nations Development

Programme, the United Nations Children's Fund and other organisations of the United Nations system, acting within their mandates, in the promotion of the human rights of women, and improve cooperation between the Division for the Advancement of Women and the Centre for Human Rights;

(h) Encourage incorporation of a gender perspective in national programmes of action and in human rights and national institutions, within the context of human rights advisory services programmes;

(i) Establish effective cooperation between the United Nation High Commissioner for Human Rights and the United Nations High Commissioner for Refugees and other relevant bodies, within their respective mandates taking into account the close link between massive violations of human rights, especially in the form of genocide, ethnic cleansing, systematic rape of women in war situations and refugee flows and other displacements, and the fact that refugee, displaced and returnee women may be subject to particular human rights abuse;

(j) Provide training in the human rights of women for all United Nations personnel and officials, especially those in human rights and humanitarian relief activities, and promote their understanding of the human rights of women so that they recognize and deal with violations of the human rights of women and can fully take into account the gender aspect of their work;

(k) In reviewing the implementation of the plan of action for the United Nations Decade for Human Rights Education (1995-2004), take into account the results of the Fourth World Conference on. Women.

Strategic Objective—Ensure Equality and Non-Discrimination Under the Law and in Practice Actions to be taken

- By Governments:

(*a*) Give priority to promoting and protecting the full and equal enjoyment by women and men of all human rights and fundamental freedoms without distinction of any kind as to race, colour, sex, language, religion, political or other opinions, national or social origins, property, birth or other status;

(*b*) Provide constitutional guarantees and/or enact appropriate legislation to prohibit discrimination on the basis of sex for all women and girls of all ages and assure women of all ages equal rights and their full enjoyment;

(*c*) Review national laws, including customary laws and legal practices in the areas of family, civil, penal, labour and commercial law in order to ensure the implementation of the principles and procedures of all relevant international human rights instruments by means of national legislation, revoke any remaining laws that discriminate of the basis of sex and remove gender bias in the administration of justice;

(*d*) Embody the principle of the equality of men and women in their legislation and ensure, through law and other appropriate means, the practical realization of this principle;

(*e*) Strengthen and encourage the development of programmes to protect the human rights of women in the national institutions on human rights that carry out programmes, such as human rights commissions or ombudspersons, according them appropriate status, resources and access to the Government to assist individuals, in particular women, and ensure that these institutions pay adequate attention to problems involving the violation of the human rights of women;

(f) Take action to ensure that the human rights of women, including the rights referred to in paragraphs 94 to 96 above, are fully respected and protected;

(g) Prohibit female genital mutilation wherever it exists and give vigorous support to efforts among non-governmental and community organisations and religious institutions to eliminate such practices,

(h) Take urgent action to combat and eliminate violence against women, which is a human rights violation, resulting from harmful traditional or customary practices, cultural prejudices and extremism.

(i) Provide gender-sensitive human rights education and training to public officials, including, inter alia, police and military personnel, corrections officers, health and medical personnel, and social workers, including people who deal with migration and refugee issues, and teachers at all levels of the educational system, and make available such education and training also to the judiciary and members of parliament in order to enable them to better exercise their public responsibilities;

(j) Establish effective mechanisms for investigating violations of the human rights of women perpetrated by any public official and take the necessary punitive legal measures in accordance with national laws;

(k) Promote the equal right of women to be members of trade unions and other professional and social organisations;

(l) Review and amend criminal laws and procedures, as necessary, to eliminate any discrimination against women in order to ensure that criminal law and procedures guarantee women effective protection against, and prosecution of, crimes directed at or disproportionately affecting women, regardless of the relationship between the perpetrator and the victim, and ensure that women defendants, victims and/or witnesses are not revictimized or discriminated against in the investigation and prosecution of crimes;

(m) Strengthen existing or establish readily available and free or affordable alternative administrative mechanisms and legal aid programmes to assist disadvantaged women seeking redress for violations of their rights;

(n) Ensure that women have the same right as men to be judges, advocates or other officers of the court, as well as police officers and prison and detention officers, among other things;

(o) Ensure that all women and non-governmental organisations and their members in the field of protection and promotion of all human rights civil, cultural, economic, political and social rights, including the right to development—enjoy fully all human rights and freedoms in accordance with the Universal Declaration of Human Rights and all other human rights instruments and the protection of national laws;

(p) Strengthen and encourage the implementation of the recommendations contained in the Standard

Rules on the Equalisation of Opportunities for Persons with Disabilities, [30] paying special attention to ensure non-discrimination and equal enjoyment of all human rights and fundamental freedoms by women and girls with disabilities, including their access to information and services in the field of violence against women, as well as their active participation in and economic contribution to all aspects of society;

(q) Encourage the development of gender-sensitive human rights programmes.

Strategic Objective-Achieve Legal Literacy

Actions to be taken

• By Governments and non-governmental organisations, the United Nations and other international organisations, as appropriate:

(a) Translate, whenever possible, into local and indigenous languages and into alternative formats appropriate for persons with disabilities and persons at lower levels of literacy, publicise and disseminate laws and information relating to the equal status and human rights of all women, including the Universal Declaration of "Human Rights, the International Covenant on Civil and Political Rights, the International Covenant on Economic, Social and Cultural Rights, the Convention on the Elimination of All Forms of Discrimination against Women, the International Convention on the Elimination of All Forms of Racial Discrimination [33] the Convention on the Rights of the Child, the Convention against Torture and Other Cruel Inhuman or Degrading Treatment or Punishment: the Declaration on the Right to Development [34], and the Declaration on

the Elimination of Violence against Women, as well as the outcomes of relevant United Nations conferences and summits and national reports to the Committee on the Elimination of Discrimination against Women;

(b) Publicise and disseminate such information in easily understandable formats and alternative formats appropriate for persons with disabilities, and persons at low levels of literacy;

(c) include information about international and regional Instruments and standards in their public information and human rights education activities and in adult education and training programmes particularly for groups such as the military, the police and other law enforcement personnel, the judiciary, and legal and health professionals to ensure that human rights are effectively protected;

(d) Disseminate information on national legislation and its impact on women, including easily accessible guidelines on how to use a justice system to exercise one's rights;

(e) Make widely available and fully publicize information on the existence of national, regional and international mechanisms for seeking redress when the human rights of women are violated;

(f) Promote education on the human and legal rights of women in school curricula at all levels of education and undertake public campaigns, including in the most widely used languages of the country, on the equality of women and men in public and private life, including their rights within the family and relevant human rights instruments under national and international law;

(*g*) Encourage, coordinate and cooperate with local and regional women's groups, relevant non-governmental organizations, educators and the media, to implement programmes in human rights education to make women aware of their human rights;

(*h*) Promote education in all countries in human rights and international humanitarian law for members of the national security and armed forces, including those assigned to United Nations peace-keeping operations, on a routine and continuing basis, reminding them and sensitising them to the fact that they should respect the rights of women at all times, both on and off duty, giving special attention to the rules on the protection of women and children and to the protection of human rights in situations of armed conflict;

(*i*) Take appropriate measures to ensure that refugee and displaced women, migrant women and women migrant workers are made aware of their human rights and of the recourse mechanisms available to them.

●●●

11

Policies, Programmes for Women Welfare

In this chapter policies and programmes for women in India has been given, which the Government of India, Ministry of Education and Social Welfare, Department of Social Welfare, discussed in the following points:

Health and Family Planning

Demographic indicators. *viz.*, female, maternal and infant mortality rates, and indicators of access to medical care, both reveal an increase in the neglect of female lives as an expendable asset. This is the only reasonable explanation for the declining sex ratio observed to persist over several decades. In our opinion, the neglect of maternity and child health serves and general public health services through over-concentration on efforts for family planning have contributed to this trend as well as defeated the ultimate objective of the family planning programme. We are entirely in agreement with the draft Fifth Five-Year Plan that integration of family planning with more positive health services like maternal and child health, and nutrition and improvement in the life expectancy of children and mothers will provide a far greater incentive to the adoption of family planning measures than the hitherto adopted negative approach. While welcoming this proposed integration, we with to offer certain suggestions wish regard to its organisation at different levels so that the objective of integration is not defeated by organisational separatism.

We recommended that:

(a) The rank of the Chief Executive for the integrated maternity and child health services, including family planning, should be upgraded to at least Additional Commissioner, so that this service does not again become subordinate to family planning. This procedure should be adopted at all levels of the administration at the Centre and the States.

(b) A separate budget head for maternity and child health services should be created, drawing on the provision now made for family planning and the general health services. It is important to increase the provision for these services to avoid their being neglected as has been the trend so far. Since programmes for immunisation and nutrition of infants yield better results when they form a part of general maternity and child health services, we see no difficulty in increasing the allocation for these services.

(c) At the level of the primary health centres, the maternity and child health service should be separated for purposes of administrative provision, medical personnel and budget. While they may share the same buildings and equipment, a separation of the administrative structure required for maternity and child health services will ensure greater priority of treatment. Facilities in the way of maternity beds, equipment for immunisation of children and family planning for women could be allocated to the MCR Unit. The P.R.C. could be made responsible for sterilisation operations for men along with other general health services.

The MCR Unit could coordinate the nutrition and immunisation measures, which form a basis component of the integrated child development programme. It could also collect and maintain fertility and morbidity statistics for women and children for better research and evaluation in these fields.

We recommend that each M.C.R. centre should collect this data, which should be studied and evaluated at the district level by persons of required competence. This will call for a health statistics Section at the district level.

(d) We recommend the abolition of the present practice of providing financial incentives to promoters of family planning. Incentives to women who accept family planning should be in the shape of a token or certificate to ensure them greater priority in health care facilities for both the mothers and their children. Such a step will promote greater acceptance of family planning and correct social attitudes towards these practices. Compensation for loss of wages during sterilisation operations should however be paid to daily wage labourers. Others should be given paid leave for this purpose.

(e) The qualifications prescribed for recruitment of personnel for these services in rural areas need to be gradually raised. Unit women of requisite higher qualifications are available, the present requirements may continue, but they should be reviewed and progressively increased after every 3 years. Attempts should also be made to obtain the services of older and mature women for these services in the rural areas.

(f) We disapprove the denial of maternity benefits to women in Government service after three children as adopted by some State Government and recommend rescinding of such orders.

(g) We further recommend the promotion of research in the field of female disorders *e.g.* puerperal psychosis and effects of family planning methods.

(h) We also recommend that mass campaigns for family planning should also aim to correct prevailing social attitudes

regarding fertility and metabolic hereditary disorders and the sex of the child for which the women is generally blamed. Correct information in these matters would go a long way to improve the status of women.

Changes Needed in the Medical Termination of Pregnancy Act

(a) According to Section 4 (a) of the Act, consent of a minor girl is not required for this operation while in other surgical operations of children above 12 such consent is necessary. In our view this distinction is uncalled for and may lead to guardians compelling young girls to undergo this operation even when they do not want it. The consent of the patient should be essential. In the case of a minor girl nearing majority, if the doctor and the patient are in agreement, the consent of the guardian may be dispensed with. In all such cases, greater discretion should be permitted to the doctor.

(b) Sections 8 of the Act provides an overriding precaution to the doctor for any damage caused by the operation. Since no such protection is given for other operations, this Beems an unnecessary clause and may lead to negligence. It may, therefore, be dropped.

(c) While we appreciate the ethical considerations, which make many doctors reluctant to perform this operation, we feel that it is a woman's right to have control over the size of her family. At the same time it is important that doctors should have the authority to discourage such operations when they pose definite risk to the health of a patient. The condition being imposed in many hospitals that abortion will only be performed if the patient agrees to sterilisation, should not be compulsive. It would be far better to adopt methods of persuasion through expert counselling.

(d) The procedure and paper work involved in these operations need to be simplified. It is also necessary to

extend facilities for authorised termination of pregnancies, particularly in the rural areas.

(e) Many hospitals continue to insist on the husband's consent before performing these operations though this is not required by the law. A special effort needs to be made to convince the medical profession of the social value of this law from the point of view both individuals and society.

(f) Most doctors are reluctant to perform these operations in the case of unmarried girls. It is necessary to clarify the point that rape is not the only ground to justify termination in cases of unmarried girls, nor is there any legal obligation on the doctor to inform the Policy of an operation done in a rape case.

Welfare and Development

In order to prevent any ambiguity in the understanding of what constitutes women's welfare and to prevent the development of policies that sometimes go against the basic objectives, we recommend that the Government of India should evolve a national policy on women's development in the light of the constitutional directives and pledges made to the women of this country and to the international community from time to time.

In view of the need to maintain links between governmental, voluntary and community effort for promotion of women's welfare and to assist the process of Government planning with actual knowledge and experiences of the problems and needs of women at different levels.

We recommend:

(a) Reorganisation of the Central Social Welfare Board as a statutory and autonomous specialised agency for planning, coordination and management of welfare and development programmes for women and children.

(b) Reorganisation of the State Welfare Advisory Boards as statutory autonomous agencies at the State level with similar functions. In addition, the State Boards may also serve as links between the Central agency, the State Government and the local bodies.

Need for Agencies for Coordination, Communication and Implementation of Measures to Improve the Status of Women.

The U.N. Commission on the Status of Women in its 25th Report has recommended establishment of a National Commission or similar bodies "with a mandate to review, evaluate and recommend measures and priorities to ensure equality between men and women and the full integration of women in all sectors of national life". We accordingly recommend the constitutions of statutory autonomous Commissions at the Centre and the State with the following functions:

(a) Collection of information on different matters, *e.g.* education, employment, health, welfare, political participation, impact of social legislation, etc., with the right to call for information on different matters from the concerned agencies of the Government and to suggest improved methods for collection of data in different fields.

(b) Evaluation of existing policies, programmes and laws that have a bearing on status of women with the following powers:

(i) The Commission's criticisms and suggestion made after due consultation with relevant Ministries or Departments of Government should be placed before Parliament or the State Legislatures. They would be answered by the Government within a states period with explanation or assurances.

(ii) To ensure non-implementation of these measures; to point out lacunae or deficiencies in such measures and suggest amendments.

(c) Recommendations of new laws, policies or programmes aiming to implement the Directive Principles of State Policy and the objectives of the U.N. Resolutions and Conventions regarding the status of women. These should be made to Parliament or the state Legislatures and Government will be statutorily responsible to consider such recommendations for action or to explain why they cannot be accepted.

(d) Redressal of grievances in cases of actual violation of existing laws.

The Commission may be empowered to take effective steps to redress the grievances of affected parties.

Composition of the Commissions

The composition of these Commissions should be broad-based, one category being selected for their representative status from different bodies like leading women's organisations, trade unions, legislatures, employers, etc., and the other group consisting of experts from the field of law, health education, social research planning and administration. The Chairmen and the majority of the members of all the Commissions should be women. The Chairmen should be non-officials, but on a full time basis.

We further recommend the establishment of special Tribunals for all violations of human rights, discrimination against women, violation or evasion of existing laws and policies for the protection of women and their rights in society.

BLUE PRINT OF ACTIONS POINTS

1. Legislative Measures

The existing legislations should be reviewed so that equality and social justice can be ensured to women of all communities and creeds. Where this involves amendments to existing personal Laws of minority group, initial efforts should be concentrated on arousing a desire for change from among the members of such minority groups. A vigorous campaign should be made to educated women about their rights, and to generate among all communities, a desire for a common civil code, to be achieved by the end of the U.N. Decade for Women in 1985.

Legal aid should be organised for women in need with the active assistance of the Bar Councils.

The setting up of family courts should be considered for speedy and effective adjudication in all cases concerning the family. Women, particularly in rural areas, should be protected against harassment.

The practice of dowry should be eradicated. The legislation should be strictly enforced. This is a social evil, which requires sustained action not only on the part of Governmental agencies, but also on the part of voluntary organisations and public leaders.

The provision of the existing Child Marriage Restraint Act should be reviewed. Special attention should be given to streamlining the enforcement machinery and involving local authorities and voluntary organisations in the implementation of the Act. Active public support should be mobilised by Governmental agencies, voluntary organisations and public leaders against child marriage, particularly in rural areas. Simultaneously, systematic programmes of education and training should be developed for girls till they marry.

2. Administrative Measures

Education

Education is the greatest known catalytic agent for social change. All out efforts should therefore be made to achieve the goal of universal primary education as early as possible. The ideas of equality between the sexes and participation by women in development should be woven into the fabric of the educational system.

The employment of women teachers should be actively promoted. The existing employment procedures, including those for part-time employment, should be reviewed and, where necessary, relaxations in age, etc., made so that more women teachers, can be employed, and husbands and wives are posted in the same schools or at the same station.

The content of education should be strengthened in terms of both life and work relevance. Attention should be given to vocationalisation and diversification of courses, which should not only be limited to traditional women's vocations but also give emphasis on the preparation of women for participation in modern sectors of industrial production. Polytechnics (including mini-polytechnics) should be started for girls in the smaller urban centres to provide training facilities in trades crafts, which will prompt self-employment.

At the stage of higher education special incentives like freeships, scholarships, hostel facilities, and book loans should be made available to girls from rural, backward and hilly areas, from backward classes and from poor families. A greater diversification in the courses offered should be made to enhance work opportunities in nontraditional vocations in modern sectors of industrial production.

Adoption of multiple entry in education, non-formal part-time education facilities condensed courses for education correspondence courses and courses for continuing education should be made available in a larger measure to women in semi-urban and rural areas, and to working women in urban and semi-urban areas. Adult education and functional literacy programmes should be vigorously pursued through both official and voluntary agencies.

3. Employment

Equal Remuneration Act, 1976, has been passed, providing for the payment of equal remuneration to men and women workers and the prevention of discrimination on grounds of sex. Special steps should therefore be taken to review recruitment, promotion another personnel practices in all public and private sector undertakings to ensure that there is no discrimination against women candidates. Women apprentices should be taken without discrimination in industries. Representatives of women's voluntary organisations should be associated in the machinery set up to ensure adequate participation of women in employment.

Village industries, which provide scope for the employment of women should be further promoted. Special training services should be organised and credit, marketing facilities, etc. extended, specially in regard to crafts which can have a ready export market, through modernisation of design, etc. Integrated pilot projects to cover training, production and marketing should be started.

The existing recruitment procedures and employment conditions should be reviewed to encourage the re-entry of women into the work force. For this purpose, the provisions relating to maximum age of entry into service should be reviewed. Part-time employment of women should be promoted wherever feasible. Refresher courses and training programmes should be organised for adult women to make them fit for re-employment.

Organisations entrusted by the Government with the task of promoting self-employment opportunities should develop special women's entrepreneurial training motivation programmes and provide special assistance to women entrepreneurs and to women's co-operative in terms of credit, licensing, etc.

The existing legislation in regard to maternity benefits should be reviewed. It should simultaneously be ensured that there is no consequent adverse effect on the employment of women.

4. Health Care, Nutrition and Family Planning

Maternal and child health care facilities should be expanded, particularly in semi-urban and rural areas, and coverage provided to high risk pregnant women. Antenatal and post-natal clinics should be started in every Primary Health Centre and district hospital.

Nutrition supplementation should be provided to high risk pregnant mothers. Simultaneously, nutrition and health education should be given to girls and to mothers through all available media and institutions (school, hospitals, PHCs, etc.)

Family welfare planning services should be expanded and measures intensified to educate and prepare couples to avail them, specifically in rural, backward and tribal areas. The facilities under the Medical Termination of Pregnancy Act, 1971 should be made available in semiurban and rural areas and information regarding the provisions disseminated among women, immunisation facilities should be gradually extended to all children.

Facilities of Working Women

The establishment of day-care centres, creches, and balwadis should be promoted on a large scale in rural, semi-urban and urban areas to help working mothers and active women social workers discharge their duties, and enable the older children to attend school.

Hostel facilities for working women of the lower income groups should be expanded.

Care for the Socially Disadvantaged

Women without any means of support, and the physically handicapped should be provided services for education, training and rehabilitation so that they can become selfreliant. Old age homes should be opened for the aged and the infirm. Special programmes should be developed for unmarried mothers and their children.

The provision of the Suppression of Immoral Traffic Act (1956) should be reviewed to facilitate their more efficient implementation. Comprehensive rehabilitation programmes for victims of immoral traffic and their children should de developed. Special steps should be taken to prevent vulnerable young girls and women from becoming victims of this social evil.

EDUCATION

1. Introduction

In realisation of the importance of education in general and the need for equality in opportunities for the intellectual development of men and women, successive Five Year Plans have consistently placed special emphasis on the acceleration of women's education. The emphasis with regard to women's education has along been to equip her for the multiple roles as citizens, house-wives, mothers, contributors to family income and builders of the new society. Efforts have been made during the past two decades of planned development to enrol more girls in school; to encourage girls to stay in schools; to continue their education as long as possible; and to provide non-formal education opportunities for women. The Draft Fifth Five-Year Plan has declared that, "the outlays for the education of girls will be stepped up.... " The fulfilment of the constitutional directive in respect of providing free and compulsory education upto the age of 14 years has been included as one of the components of the Minimum Needs Programme.

These efforts have had a significant impact on the progress of women's education in India. For example, there is a primary school within the easy walking distance from the home of almost all the children. This has resulted in an increase in the enrolment of girls in classes I-V as a percentage of total enrolment in these classes. In respect of classes I-VIII, IX, XII, XII and university education also there has been an appreciable increase in the percentage of girls' enrolment to total enrolment. In fact, girls' enrolment is observed to be growing at a faster rate then those of boys.

Despite these encouraging trends and marked progress made in respect of women's education, the education status of women is still far from satisfactory for the following reasons:

(a) Literacy among women is generally lower than that among men. According to the 1971 Census data, only 13.4 percent of women in this age-group of 25+ are literate. According to 2001 census 62.3 percent of women in the age group of 25 + are literate.

(b) Enrolment of girls in classes I to V is only 66.4 percent of girls in the corresponding age-group, *i.e.* 6 to 11 years; while in repect of boys the relevant percentage is 100.2.

(c) Drop-out rate is also very high in classes I to V. A recent study has shown that the drop-out rate especially accentuated in the case of girls from rural areas and from the less privileged sections of society, is as heavy as 42.85 percent between classes I and II.

(d) In classes VI to VIII, percentages of enrolment of girls and boys to the total girls and boys in the

relevant age-group (*i.e.* 11 to 14 years) are 22.2 and 48.3, respectively.

(e) At the secondary stage, *i.e.* classes IX to XIIXII girls enrolled constitute only 12 percent of girls in the relevant age-group 14 to 17 years as against 31 percent in respect of the enrolment of boys in this age-group.

(f) Enrolment of girls in Post-Matric classes constitutes only 2.3 percent of girls in the concerned age-group 17 to 23 years, while the enrolment percentage of boys in this age-group is 7.5.

2. Factors Retarding the Progress of Women's Education

Girls and women in India have thus not been able to take full advantage of the available opportunities/facilities for intellectual development. This is mainly because of several social and cultural factors in addition to various other reasons. Action plans and strategies for women's education should, therefore, aim at neutralising the effects of the factors, which have retarded the progress of women's education in India. With a view to facilitating the formulation of such a plan of action, in what follows, some of the major reasons which have operated against girls/women in taking full advantage of educational opportunities/facilities are listed below:

(a) General indifference to education of girls.

(b) Social resistance arising out of fears and misconceptions that education might alienate girls from traditions and social values and lead to mal-adjustments, conflicts and non-conformism.

(c) Early marriage and social inhibitions against girls pursuing education after marriage.

(d) Prevalence of child labour among girls belonging to weaker sections and the hard domestic chores which

some of the unmarried girls—even in the middle class families—are required to perform.

(e) Discrimination effected by employers against women labour in both organised and unorganised sectors in matters of recruitment, training and promotion.

(f) The prevailing notion that the sole occupation of women is to bear children, look after her husband and children, and thus be restricted to domestic work.

(g) Many girls and their parents find that the school curriculum do not conform adequately to their needs and interests.

(h) Unsuitable and inflexible school timings and inadequate facilities for girls in schools, particularly in the co-educational schools.

3. Major Objective of Women's Education

It should be recognised here that the general objective of any policy towards women's education cannot be different from those relating to men. However, in view of the social and cultural handicaps that have operated against women in general and in view of the multiple role that women are required to play, the need for a set of objectives specific to women's education is imperative. The following major objectives are, therefore, considered here:

(a) Prepare women to fully participate in socially productive work, fully aware of family planning needs with a view to achieving her full integration with the democratic and developmental efforts of the country.

(b) Help break down over covert biases against women.

(c) Make women aware of the various legal, social and economic rights, provisions and privileges available

to them and the way they can take advantage of them, for their advancement.

(*d*) Import the idea of equality between the sexes and participation by women in development through the educational system.

(*e*) Enable women to be self-reliant to achieve economic independence.

(*f*) And above all, to find full expression for her talent, ability and personality and for this purpose, enable her to adopt a discriminating attitude so that she can escape the bonds of superstition and obscurantism.

4. Action Plans

Action plans here are evolved within the general framework of major objectives mentioned above. In addition, the action plans have taken into consideration other objectives, which are specific of educational categories like elementary education, middle stage education, secondary stage education, middle stage education and non-formal education. For the sake of convenience, in what follows, action plans specific of each age-groups of girls, are all mentioned separately.

A. Elementary Education for Girls in the Age-Group 6-11 Years

Girls in this age-group constitute the population of girls of primary school going age. Action plans for this age-group will need to be in two directions:

(*a*) To universalise primary education for girls, and

(*b*) To strive for the retention of girls already enrolled.

Towards this end, the following action plans are suggested:

Administrative and Structural Measures

(i) State Governments should take note of the habitations without primary schools as indicated by the Third Educational Survey and make arrangements for providing primary school within a distance of 1.5 kms. of all habitations within next five years.

(ii) Girls in this age are often required to look after younger children and attend minor household duties, particularly in the rural areas and among the weaker sections of the society. As this is one of the major reasons that holds such girls from attending school, special efforts should be made to enlarge the scope and coverage of pre-school education programmes like balwadis and anganwadis, where the older girls can be given practical work experience and child care.

(iii) Mobile schools should be provided for children of all nomadic tribes, migrant labour and construction workers.

(iv) These pre-school education programmes should wherever possible, be attached to primary schools or at least located in the vicinity of primary schools, as that would help in cultivating a school going habit right from the childhood.

(v) Supervision and inspection of primary schools should give particular attention to the problem of enrolment of girls, their retetion, involvement of the community, etc.

Promotional and Motivational Measures

(vi) Special and sustained persuasive and motivational campaign and organisational drives should be

undertaken among regions/communities which have shown markedly a low achievement in girls enrolment. Voluntary organisations at local level like Mahila Mandals and local bodies should be fully involved in this programme.

(vii) Promotion and support to girls' education should also be tackled through a multi-pronged programme of incentives—both for bringing girls to schools and for retaining them in schools. The incentives can be in the form of mid-day meals, free supply of books and reading materials, scholarships awards, etc.

Pedagogical Measures

(viii) The primary teacher training course should undergo a major revision with a view to adequately preparing the teacher for the promotion of girls' education. Emphasis should be more on the use of such non-formal methods of imparting education that would interest and attract more and more girls to attend schools.

B. Education for Girls in the Age-Group 11-14 Years

Population of girls in this age-group constitutes girls of middle school-going age. This group can be divided into three sub-groups:

(a) Girls students attending middle schools;

(b) Girl drop-outs at various stages from Class I to V;

(c) Girls who have never attended schools.

The objectives of education and training are different for each of the sub-groups.

(a) Middle School-Girl Students

Action plans for education of girls in this age-group should be concerned about:

(i) encouraging further enrolment of girls at this stage,

(ii) retention of girls already is middle schools, and

(iii) rendering the curriculum more relevant.

The following action plans are suggested:

Pedagogical Measures

(i) The content should be more oriented to the needs of girls in the village communities so that both the parents and the girls see relevance of this education for their own lives. The curriculum of the middle school stage needs to be given a strong work experience orientation, introducing girls to crafts and skills which will be of direct use to them in the family, community and farm, and help them in rural employment and self-employment.

(ii) *Women Teachers:* It is important for the promotion of girls' education to employ women teachers in schools. In fact, the general view is that women are more suited to be teachers and larger number of teachers should be women. However, the problem may come up in different ways. More number of men may be qualified and trained women may be not be in a position to accept employment as full time teachers due to personal problems; women also have difficulties in working in rural areas. There has to be relaxation from age restrictions. The States may consider reserving a certain number of posts of teachers for women and where there are not adequate number of trained teachers, untrained persons may be recruited and deputed for training.

It may also be worth while in those areas which have schools without women teachers, to select educated women in that area and send them for training and appoint them in the schools in that area. Where educated women are not available for posting in a school, local women may be selected and posted as school matas (school mothers) to keep the girl students company and induce parents to send their girls and children to schools. The rules relating to age and qualification of recruitment and service may have to be relaxed in these cases and the deficiency made up through in-service training. The question of giving posting to husband and wife both of whom are teachers int he same place may be considered.

Women should not be discriminated against in matters of recruitment. Selection and recruitment should be made on merit. No qualified meritorious woman candidate should be' over looked. State Governments may contemplate providing for 50 percent of teachers in schools being women and to look into this aspect while sanctioning grants to institutions.

(iii) The primary teacher training course needs to undergo a major revision to adequately prepare the trainees for their special responsibility for the promotion of girls education in rural areas, especially in adapting the content to suit the needs and interests of girls, in adopting non-formal methodologies and in linking with community and developmental activities.

(iv) Supervision and inspection of schools should give particular attention to the problem of enrolment of girls, their retention, factors contributing to wastage and stagnation, relevation of curriculum, involvement of the community, working conditions of women teachers, etc.

Promotional and Motivational Measures

(v) School timings should be flexible, as many of the girls in this age-group are required to help their mothers in routine domestic chores.

(vi) Incentives like mid-day meals, scholarships, free school uniforms, free books and study materials, stipend, awards, etc., should be extended to all girls in the rural areas and slums in the urban areas.

(vii) Adoption of multiple entry and part-time course is recommended.

(b) *Middle School-Girl Drop-outs*

Alternative Measures

(viii) For School drop-outs of girls, pre-vocational training programmes should be organised on an extensive scale to cover all girls in the rural areas and in the slums of urban areas. The objectives of such training should be to render them self-sufficient in home management, and help them to achieve economic independence. With this in view, such training programmes should include courses in sewing, knitting, cooking, nutrition, minor repairs of the house, motherhood, child care, etc.

(c) *Girls Who Never Attended Schools*

(ix) For the non-student girls in this age-group, the objective should be to provide adequate preparation in life through a combined three-year course in general education and vocational training. Vocational training should be on the lines of pre-vocational training mentioned above.

(x) Such training programmes should be extended to all girls in the rural areas. In the urban areas, preference

should be given to girls in slum areas and destitute girls.

C. Education for Girls in the Age-Group 14-17 Years

4.4 Girls in this age-group also can be classified into three groups:

(a) Girl students with motivation to attend secondary school;

(b) Non-student girls, *i.e.*, students who never attended schools.

(c) Girl drop-outs from classes VI to VIII.

(a) Girl Students

The action plans under this category should emphasise more on:

(i) facilitating more girls to pursue education at the secondary stage, and

(ii) strengthening the content in terms of both life and work relevance.

The following action plans are suggested:

Administrative and Structural Measures

(i) Separate girls schools or separate sections should be started where the social/cultural environment demands them.

(ii) In co-education schools special attention should be given to the provision of adequate toilet, rest and recreation facilities, separately for girls.

(iii) State Governments, which have not yet made high school education free for girls should do so on a priority basis.

(iv) Multiple entry system and part-time education may be provided.

Promotional and Motivational Measures

(v) All courses of training in vocational and technical schools at the secondary stage should be open to both boys and girls. There should be no discrimination in this regard.

(vi) Liberal incentives in the form of book allowances, book-bank facilities, etc., should be extended to encourage more girls in rural areas and backward areas to pursue secondary education.

(vii) Separate hostel facilities should be provided particularly in rural areas and residential scholarships should be offered.

Pedagogical Measures

(viii) The curriculum should be more diversified taking into consideration the various occupational opportunities available, to women and the interests and aptitudes of girls.

(b) Girl Drop-outs

Alternative Measures

(ix) Condensed courses of education started in 1958 were found very useful. Under this scheme women in the age-group 13-30 years who have had some schooling are prepared for middle school, matriculation or equivalent examinations within a period of 2 years' duration. The minimum age limit here should be reduced to 15 years. This scheme should be extended to cover all rural areas and weaker sections of the urban community.

(x) The condensed course should be organised for smaller groups, say 5 to 7 persons, using the community resources like girls' high schools and girls' colleges.

(xi) Correspondence courses and self-study programmes may be introduced.

(xii) Apart from imparting general education, condensed course should also aim imparting job-oriented training with the active cooperation of existing vocational training institutions.

(xiii) Efforts should be made to cover at least about 215 lakhs of girls in the age-group 15-30 under the condensed courses programme during the Fifth Plan period.

(c) Non-student Girls

(xiv) Fourth Plan introduced a programme of functional literacy with the objective of imparting elementary general education and vocational training-related to the functions performed-to men and women in the rural areas who never attended schools. This programme should be expanded to cover all rural areas.

(xv) Apart from imparting general elementary education and knowledge about farming techniques, the curriculum for women should include courses of training in occupational skills like kitchen, gardening, food processing, poultry keeping, animal husbandry; household arts like cooking nutritional values of foods locally available, sewing, knitting etc., and motherhood, child care and family planning as also electronics and like fields.

(*xvi*) Similar programmes should also be designed for girls in this age-group and under this category belonging to urban areas.

D. Education for Girls in the Age-Group 17 Years and Above

4.5 Education for girls in this age group also can be divided into three groups, as in the case of other age-groups:

(*a*) Education of girls at the higher education stage.

(*b*) Education for non-student girls-girls who who never had any education.

(*c*) Education for girl drop-outs from the educational system beyond the secondary stage.

In respect of the last category here, the education for non-student girls, action plans are the same as those concerning non-student girls in the age-group 14-17 years. Hence, this category is not dealt with separately here.

(a) Education for Girls at the Higher Education Stage

Action plans in this area should aim at:

(a) Making the curriculum more relevant and responsive to the cultural and occupational needs of women.

(b) Making higher education available to the less privileged sections of the society, particularly girls from the rural areas.

The following action plans may be taken up for consideration:

Administrative and Structural Measures

(*i*) The general policy here should be to discourage separate institutions for women and to promote coeducational facilities. However, in areas where separate institutions are required to promote education of women, they may be permitted on the merits of such cases.

(ii) Vocational counselling and guidance services should be organised in a more meaningful way to help girls-in college and universities-opt for suitable courses relevant to their talent, interests and needs.

Promotional and Motivational Measures

(iii) Incentives like scholarships, freeships, etc., should be provided to enable girls from rural areas to pursue highl education.

(iv) Provision of self-cooking facilities in hostels for girls should also be considered.

(v) For girls belonging to weaker sections, in-addition to freeships and scholarships, bursaries should also be provided to meet their expenses on food and lodging.

(vi) Girls pursuing higher education should be provided easy access to text-books and other reference material through book-bank facilities.

(viii) Girls should be encouraged to enter professional courses. If necessary, reservation of seats for girls in professional courses may be considered.

Pedagogical Measures

(viii) Diversification of courses at the junior college level and undergraduate level should be undertaken on a priority basis with a view to preparing the girls for the various employment opportunities open to them.

(b) *Education for Girl Drop-outs*

Girls in this age-group drop-out of educational system for various reasons. Marriage is one of the reasons, which force girls in this age-group to discontinue further formal education. Economic hardship is another reason, which forces some girls to a drop-out and seek jobs, with a view to supporting their families. Social prejudices and cultural attitudes also force some of the girls to leave the formal educational system. For girls in this category, therefore, the policy should be to extend non-formal educational facilities on a large scale.

The following action plans are suggested:

(i) Facilities for part-time self-study and correspondence courses should be expanded on a large scale to enable working girls and non-working-married and unmarried girls to enhance their educational qualifications.

(ii) In addition to course leading to degree/diploma, short courses in specific subjects through summer schools/sessions, ad hoc programmes like seminars, laboratory work, workshop experience, etc., should be organised for working· girls, with a view to upgrading their professional skills and qualifications. Facilities for further education not necessarily leading to a degree, but for upgradation of knowledge and skills could be provided.

(iii) While the initiative for organising such programmes should be taken by the Central and State Governments, the employees should also be increasingly involved.

(iv) Entrepreneurship development programmes should be organised separately for educated women in the age-group 18-30 years with an minimum of matriculation level of education.

(v) Pre-examination training facilities should be orgnaised on a large scale for educated women

from the rural areas and those belonging to weaker sections with the objective of equipping them to successfully compete in examinations for public jobs.

The objective of such training programmes should be:

(a) Make them aware of the various opportunities for self-employment;

(b) Motivate them to take up self-employment;

(c) Impart needed skills/training; and

(d) Promote achievement motivation among them.

E. Administrative Measures

To make the various action plans successful and to achieve a real breakthrough in women's education, there is urgent need for a matching and effective administrative set up, both at the central and state levels. With this in view, the following suggestions are made:

(i) In the Union Ministry of Education and Social Welfare, a special unit/cell may be setup to be in charge of women's education to review and initiate follow-up action.

(ii) In each State education department, a senior officer should be placed in charge of girls' education in order that it may receive adequate emphasis, execution and co-ordination.

(iii) As the district is the operational unit for all educational programmes and as the needs of girls vary in extent and kind from area to area within a district, a separate cell for girls' education-formal and non-formal-may be created within the purview of the district educational officer at the district headquarters.

(iv) School supervisory system should be staffed with more women.

(v) A suitable machinery may be set up at the Centre and the States to help in the formulation of plans for women's education-formal and non-formal to monitory, co-ordinate and evaluate progress of women's education from time to time, to create public opinion in favour of women's education etc.

Report of Working Group on Employment of Women (set up by the Planning Commission), September 1978. Government of India, Department of India, Department of Social Welfare, Women's Welfare and Development Bureau, New Delhi

In the context of the preparation of the Sixth Five Year Plan, the Planning Commission set up a Working Group on Employment of women to examine ways and means of increasing the employment of women. The Group scrutinised statistics on women's existing programmes/schemes of the Government pertaining to women, development of self-employment and enterpreneurship among women, skill development, and development of Cadres for promoting employment of women.

Their findings indicated that the problems of women's employment were characterised by *(i)* The inability of women to reach for services and assistance programmes offered by government and semi-government institutions; *(ii)* A lack of awareness among institutions about the need to promote employment of women; *(iii)* The tendency of economically powerful organisations to obtain financial and other assistance in the name of women but diverting it to other areas of investment; and *(iv)* The failure of technological modernisation of several industries in expanding employment opportunities for women, widening of skill training opportunities, and upward mobility of women workers.

The Group recommended earmarking of funds in sectoral plans; increasing their participation in decision-making processes; and collecting of micro-level data on employment conditions, unemployment situation and skill profile of local women, amongst others.

Development of Village Level Organisations: Report of the Working Group on Development of Village Level Organisation of Rural Women, June 1987, Government of India, Ministry of Agriculture and Irrigation, Department of Rural Development, New Delhi

A Working Group was constituted by the Department of Rural Development with two-fold purposes. One of the purpose was to review the objectives and functioning of associate organisation. Mahila Mandals and Youth clubs as well as their links with other agencies. The second purpose was to make recommendations on the basis of the findings especially about programmes to be implemented through the organisation, coordination with the work of other agencies, association of weaker sections with the associate organisations, and strengthening the cadre of workers or extension agents.

For detailed deliberations three sub-groups were constituted. These included sub-groups on the needs of rural women, objectives of Mahila Mandals and their involvement in rural development; sub-group on rural youth, their promotion, strengthening and training for participation in rural development programmes; and subgroup on block, district and state level functionaries for women's programmes and their training.

The report was submitted in two parts. Part I dealt with village level organisations for rural women including indicators of neglect, assessment of existing programme, new programmes, implications, and so forth. Part II dealt with development of rural youth organisation particularly to promote and strengthen. Yuvak Mandals.

Index